T0208735

Sandra and Me

Phyllis Strickland

Foreword by Reverend Dennis Marshall, Bethlehem
United Methodist Church, Claremont, NC

WESTBOW
PRESS®
A DIVISION OF THOMAS NELSON
& ZONDERVAN

WestBow Press books may be ordered through booksellers or by contacting:

WestBow Press
A Division of Thomas Nelson & Zondervan
1663 Liberty Drive
Bloomington, IN 47403
www.westbowpress.com
1 (866) 928-1240

ISBN: 978-1-9736-5439-1 (sc)
ISBN: 978-1-9736-5441-4 (hc)
ISBN: 978-1-9736-5440-7 (e)

Library of Congress Control Number: 2019902804

Print information available on the last page.

WestBow Press rev. date: 03/06/2019

Dedicated to the family of Sandra Miller, whose devotion during her illness was, and remains, unparalleled. Rest assured, the support and affection you showed during this difficult time did not go unnoticed. She loved each of you dearly. May her spirit guide and comfort you through life.

Special thanks to Pat and Kay, whose friendship completed our circle leading to many happy memories; to my Aunt Lottie, for her gentle words; and to the stranger in the furniture store, for pushing me forward.

Always cherish the memories.

Contents

Foreword

What better way to commemorate someone's life than to have that task taken up by a person's best friend. Expressed in the pages of this book, Phyllis Strickland shares her memories of a lifetime friendship spent with her best friend, Sandra Miller. They were friends from a very early age until Sandra's last moments of life. This book serves as the fulfillment of a promise made to Sandra that their lifetime spent together would be written down to offer to all who knew this special lady a glimpse of parts of her life they may not have known.

I want to thank Phyllis for allowing me this great honor. As a Pastor, I seldom get to offer my remembrances of someone outside the funeral setting, and often times that does not allow a justifiable amount of time to honor a person like Sandra Miller.

I was starting my eighteenth year of pastoral ministry and had just been appointed to Bethlehem United Methodist Church in Claremont, North Carolina. It was a great appointment for me and for the congregants of Bethlehem. I needed to be closer to my mother, who lives less than 30 miles away, and was in declining health. Bethlehem needed someone who could help them grow in attendance. The congregation had been experiencing several years of declining attendance due mostly to the aging of the members.

The most difficult task in starting a new appointment is learning how the Church lives and breathes in as little time as you can. It did not take me long to realize that at the very heartbeat of the life of Bethlehem was a lady named Sandra Miller. I noticed quickly that she made most everything happen and was involved in nearly every facet of the Church's routine, from Communion Steward to preparing a meal for the local high school's football team on home game nights. None of us at Church realized the impact Sandra made on the life of the Church until after her demise. Sandra did each and every one of these tasks without drawing attention to herself and without the need for gratitude or the expectation of it.

I came to rely heavily on her faithful service and had to make sure I didn't take advantage of it. You know, the tendency is to delegate tasks to the one who is already doing all the work because you know it will get done. I remember one task in particular that the Church was asked to provide by the principal of our local high school. The school year had just started when tragedy struck our entire community. Two students were killed in a car accident. Their funerals were scheduled on the same day at different Churches and at different times. The first was scheduled in the morning, and the other for later that afternoon. The principal had asked if we could provide a meal for the students between the services. The high school provided the students the day off from school and agreed to bus them to the services, but according to state law, they could not bus them back to school for lunch. I immediately asked Sandra if we could provide this service. I was so afraid that I may have overstepped my boundary and expected too much. Her first response was, "How many are we talking about feeding?" I was very hesitant to reply even though I knew exactly what the answer was to her question. I reluctantly told her the number may be between four to five hundred. I will never forget her response. She said, "Call the principal back and tell him we'll be glad to take care of it. They (the students) need to know we love and support them during this time." To this day I still do not know how she pulled that seemingly impossible task off, but she most certainly did. It was a true testament of a faith that we can do all things through Christ's strength.

Sandra's faith in Christ was more than spoken words. She lived out her faith as well. There's no greater truth to that way of life than the evidence you find in someone's family. Sandra was not only viewed by her Church family as an example of what it means to be a Christian, but it was obvious she had passed on not only her faith in our Savior, but her servant's heart to her children and grandchildren as well. Sandra was very proud of her family and she had every right to be. If the Church doors are open, each and every one of them are in attendance. And like their mother, if they are asked to serve, they do so without hesitation.

The Pastoral ministry is a wonderful way of life. A Pastor is afforded the opportunity to be in almost every part of parishioners' lives from day cares to graduations, and marriages to births, and yes, even near the time of death. I can still see Sandra's face when she told me that she had cancer. It was a momentary look of fear which was immediately followed by the look of faith and determination that I had witnessed so many times. She tackled treatment with the same work ethic she had for everything she did. When we heard the results of the treatment, and they were not promising, it devastated all of us. Then we are informed that there is no other treatment possible. We prayed. A few days later, the doctor tells of a treatment that he had discovered that might work. It was good news and bad. He said that treatment may prolong life, but would not cure the cancer, and the side effects would not render a good quality of life. It was one of the saddest moments I have ever had in ministry.

A couple of days after that, Sandra was in the hospital and I went to visit. On my way there, I had hoped that she and I could have a moment alone. A decision had not been made about the treatment the doctor had mentioned, and I knew Sandra would want to talk about it with me. As only God can do, when I got to her room, only Sandra and one of her daughters were there. So we engaged in normal small talk. Sandra was happy as always. She never showed any signs of anger for having cancer, or sadness for that matter. She was a pillar of faith and hope through all of it. Somehow the topic of the proposed treatment entered the conversation. That led to talking about the side effects of it. Sandra said, in a very nonchalant way, that she did not want to lose her hair. And being the comedian that I am, and that I'm losing my hair naturally, I told her that was not all that bad, and I leaned my head over so as to reveal the hairless top of it. Even to this day, I tear up when I remember her response. Even though we seemed to be making light of it, she placed her hand on my left arm and said in a very matter of fact, calming manner, "But it looks good on you." She wasn't saying it to say it would not look good on her. I knew that what she meant is she did not want me to look down on myself because I was balding. Given her situation at the time, she still found a way to minister to someone else. Sandra Miller was the epitome of grace.

Soon after that Sandra and I had our time alone to talk. The decision had to be made about the treatment. She had made her decision but was questioning herself about it. She told me that she did not want to take the treatment, and she was worried about how the family would receive it. She said she was torn between her family thinking that she was giving up the fight and the quality of life the side effects would bring. She said she was willing to fight but she did not want them to remember her as sick from cancer treatment. So we weighed the pros and cons, and she decided not to take the treatment. I told her that I would continue to pray for God to heal her, and that I would continue to do so until the very last moment.

The cancer seemed to move quickly in the weeks to follow. Sandra was moved to a hospice facility, and all of us stood by her bedside throughout that time. We laughed. We cried sometimes. We shared food and drink. I stood by and listened as the family shared stories about life together. And I was also made privy to some of the escapades between Phyllis and Sandra. I won't share any those. I'm sure you can glean those from the pages of this book.

I do, however, want to share my last conversation with Sandra Miller. The cancer had taken its toll on Sandra, and we were all realizing her battle with it was nearly finished. She was getting very weak. In a very tender moment, the family and I gathered hand-in-hand around her bed. Eddie, Sandra's son-in-law, sang a song, and we all prayed. When we finished praying and everyone said "Amen", we instinctively looked at Sandra. She had barely spoken in days, and with her eyes closed still, she followed with an "Amen" of her own. It was truly a God-given moment. After that moment, I asked the family if I could have moment alone with Sandra, and they graciously obliged. You see, even though I knew where Sandra stood with Christ, I believe it my pastoral duty to have a conversation with someone nearing death about their salvation. So, I told her, "Sandra, I wouldn't be much of a pastor if I didn't ask you if there's anything you need to make right with Christ." She leaned her head towards me with her eyes still closed and mustered, "I'm ready." I have to tell you that tears welled up in my eyes. They were tears of joy and sadness all at the same time. I told her that I had not stopped praying for God to heal her. Sandra reached her hand over and touched my arm like she did before. Her eyes opened up. She looked at me and said in a most comforting voice, "He did!" "I don't want to leave my family, but I can't wait to see Him."

I was blessed to be her pastor, and that blessing was not because of all the work and ministry she did. I consider it a blessing to have known the person she was.

And all of God's people said, "AMEN!"

Reverend Dennis B. Marshall
Bethlehem United Methodist Church
Claremont, NC

In the Beginning

In August 1947 my grandfather, a Pentecostal Holiness preacher, was reassigned from a church in Buffalo Ridge, Virginia, to pastor a church in Newton, a small town in the Piedmont section of North Carolina. On moving day, movers were scurrying about at breakneck speed, tossing boxes of breakable items without care, while ladies of the church were scrubbing cabinets and carefully lining the shelves with yellow-flowered shelf liner. It was chaotic. At the age of four, amid this turmoil, I was banished to the outdoors with orders to remain there—mainly for my safety and so I would not slow down this madness.

Wandering around our new backyard, absorbing unfamiliar surroundings, I spotted a little girl, seemingly my age, holding a doll in her left hand, standing at the edge of the field separating our homes. Slowly, one step at a time, we eased toward each other, locked eyes and simultaneously spoke those five words that would seal an enduring friendship: "Do you want to play?"

Little did we know this was the beginning of a lifelong journey. Together, we would share the fun, mischief, and playtime of our early childhood. We would skip merrily through our adolescence, delighting in our adventures and overcoming teenage tragedies. We would enter adulthood, marry, and raise and educate our children while carving out careers. With all this behind us, we would move cautiously into old age and discover the joys of senior citizenship—grandchildren, day trips, eating at places other than MacDonald's, 10 percent discounts just for making it this far, and finally dressing for comfort before style. Through it all, we would lean on each other for guidance and support. We would experience life's lessons together and honor each other's secrets until death.

Sandra spent her life in the town that raised us and even after marriage settled only a few miles from her childhood home. After marrying, I moved away, never losing touch with my best friend and exchanging visits as often as possible. Eventually my family relocated to Charlotte, only one hour away, and for the next forty-eight years, we enjoyed road trips, lake visits, our children's weddings, and the births of our grandchildren—all the while assembling our book of memories.

We never considered being without one another. We did speak of growing old together but without fear of death. We just assumed we would sit in rocking chairs on our front porches, rehashing the "good old days" for eternity.

So I was completely unprepared when my cell phone rang one crisp fall morning. En route to the grocery store, I noticed Sandra's name on the screen, and since we were earnestly trying to solidify a date for our Christmas get-together, I quickly answered. It's a conversation forever lodged in my memory.

Me: "Hey! What are you doing?"

Sandra: "Well, I just left the doctor's office."

Me: "Good. I've been telling you to get that lingering pain in your legs checked out. What did he say?"

Sandra: A brief silence, then in a broken voice, she simply stated, "I have cancer."

Me: "I'll be right there."

I remained in the grocery store parking lot for quite some time. Unbelievably, it was Sandra who was calming *me* down. "You don't need to come today. I'm tired, and I want to enjoy our time when you come. Besides, I have doctor appointments for the next two days. It's bone cancer, so I'll be seeing a specialist."

Then she added, "Please don't tell anyone. You are the first person I called, and I want us to deal with it first." I understood her meaning. We had faced lesser tragedies before, and we always needed to contemplate, discuss, and plan.

A few days later, we had our last outing together. Sandra was already dependent on a walker but, buoyed by the visit, assured me she felt well enough for lunch. Afterward, we rode through the county visiting our old haunts as she brought me up to date on landmarks torn down or repurposed, who had passed away recently, and any interesting gossip. There was never a lack of gossip in our hometown.

We discussed how this disease was progressing, how the family was dealing with the news, but also how she dreaded the sympathy she knew was coming. She vowed to be a good fighter but didn't care to know the prognosis. "I'm not going on the internet. That is your job," she said, "so just let me know if I need to do something differently." She assured me she had faith in her doctors.

Parked in front of our old high school, now transformed into administrative offices, we recounted how intimidating this stately structure seemed when we entered its doors as freshmen. Now it stood humbly before us guarding our memories, secrets, and misadventures. During our reminiscing, Sandra interjected, "It's been quite a journey, and you know, this could be our last journey together. I need you to be there with me."

I cried all the way home, not believing this could happen. Sure, I got on the internet, searching for any inkling of good news, praying for some miracle drug or glimmer of hope. And there were promising results, but later we found the cancer was stemming from the lungs and spreading quickly through her body.

Prayers and well-wishes were pouring in. Sandra was a dedicated church member, a community and charity volunteer, and a compassionate friend to all. Now everyone whose lives she had touched raced to offer support, prayers, and encouragement. Extended stays at the hospital led to rehab, then home, back to rehab, and then hospice. On March 11, 2015, just a few months after diagnosis, Sandra succumbed to this terrible disease.

Her husband and children were incredibly dedicated and

determined that Sandra would never be left alone without someone close being with her. I spent many days and nights making the drive to sit with her. She would wake during the night and spend time talking until she could again fall asleep. We both knew, without saying, that these were treasured times.

Even when we privately conceded the end was coming, we were still not comfortable or courageous enough to discuss the inevitable. Suddenly one night, Sandra, the courageous one, said, "We need to plan my funeral, you know, just in case."

Having lost her parents and a couple of siblings, she knew her death would be traumatizing for her family, and she wanted to relieve the burden as much as possible. So over the next days and weeks, as we felt we could deal with it, Sandra and I made funeral arrangements—just in case.

Nothing elaborate, she explained. That just wasn't her. Selecting the songs brought the greatest joy along with the most indecision. We would have sung the entire Baptist hymnal but unfortunately had to cut the selection process dramatically. "Sheltered in the Arms of God" was a longtime favorite of Sandra's. She selected "Because He Lives" to be dedicated to her children with an explanation that the words would help them through this difficult time and provide guidance throughout their lives. She also asked her son-in-law, an excellent vocalist, to perform a solo of his choosing but only if he agreed; it was his call. He graciously obliged with two beautiful songs.

The recessional selection was the most difficult. Sandra insisted on an uplifting exit—not a slow funeral hymn leaving the congregation in tears. She wanted the audience to participate and feel joy as she left this earth and went on to collect her reward in heaven. We sifted through a multitude of songs – finally narrowing the choices to "When We All Get to Heaven," "By and By," and "I'll Fly Away." We eventually settled on "I'll Fly Away," which proved to be a wise selection. She left the church with the choir and audience singing loud and upbeat! There were even some high fives.

But the last thing Sandra asked me to do was give a eulogy. There

4

were others who would speak and ministers who would deliver sermons, but my instructions were different. Tell the stories, make them laugh, share our journey with the congregation, and her most pointed instruction: "Now, don't you get up there and make anyone cry! Share our adventures," she said. "Let them know we were blessed, and please, please, don't *you* ever forget. Find a way to preserve the memories."

The biggest problem I faced was selecting the stories; there were so many, but time allowed for just a few. I hope she liked the ones I chose.

In retrospect, Sandra was correct to give me those instructions; it was as if she were clairvoyant or had already captured a heavenly sixth sense. The stories were well received by the congregation, and suddenly a sad occasion was filled with laughter, just as she intended. Someone said to me after the service that it was just the right amount of levity at the right time. I have a feeling Sandra knew precisely how this would play out and planned it accordingly.

During the reception following the service, it was suggested the stories should be put into print to assure the memories were immortalized. I simply nodded my appreciation and stored the thought somewhere in my mind. The first couple of years after Sandra's death were a struggle, and I was in no condition to accept the challenge. What I missed most? Not having her here to talk and laugh about the fun times. Or I would suddenly remember other adventures, but she was not here to ask, "Remember that time …?" And I missed making new memories.

Two things happened that changed my mind about the suggestion and nudged me forward.

Shortly after the Christmas holidays, I received a phone call from my Aunt Lottie—a resilient, wise Christian lady residing in Asheville, North Carolina, with a keen outlook on life. During the conversation, I expressed my inability to overcome this grief. She listened quietly before offering her thoughts.

Earlier, she had been humming an old hymn, "What a Friend We Have in Jesus," as she was vacuuming the residue from the recently removed Christmas tree. "You know, you are not without a close friend. Jesus is your friend and always will be. You can tell him anything, but you need to consider this: has it occurred to you that he put you and Sandra in each other's life for a reason? He knew she would need you at the end as both of you needed each other throughout life."

"But why her first?" I asked.

She replied, "It is not for us to wonder why. There is a reason."

That conversation with my aunt gave me a new perspective but also started me thinking that I might be missing a lesson from this tragedy. The feeling grew that I had not fulfilled my promise to preserve the memories.

Shortly after my conversation with Aunt Lottie, I was in the Newton area visiting one of the large furniture outlets when a stranger approached, tapped me on the shoulder, and asked, "I don't mean to intrude, but by chance did you know Sandra Miller?" When I replied yes, he went on to say he'd attended the funeral and been inspired by the eulogy and how fitting it was for such a sad time. Then he added, "So what have you done to preserve the memories?"

Suddenly I felt remiss. I had neglected my commitment to preserve the memories, which was Sandra's intention. Without someone to continually share memories with, they will fade and over time will disappear. As Sandra accepted life's final journey, she understood that even though we all die eventually, the memories will live forever when immortalized in print.

So even though I'd been delinquent in meeting her challenge, I finally began the quest of putting ink to paper. Now I was not limited by time at a podium but only by words, which enabled me to add more background to the stories. The more I wrote, the more stories I remembered, forcing me to always keep a notepad handy— including the bedside table for the times I woke in the middle of the night recalling a new adventure.

Writing this book, although at times difficult, has been a healing process and a way to enjoy again the good times we shared by now sharing them with others, perhaps bringing joy, comfort, and hopefully a laugh or two. But most of all it has meant completing Sandra's challenge to me: making sure our memories live forever.

During her illness, with all the pain and suffering, I was most impressed by Sandra's courage. She never complained and welcomed all who visited, being a great hostess until the end. I have often wondered whether I would have had the courage to plan my funeral and keep a spirited outlook on life, or whether I would have just wallowed in self-pity. She fought throughout her illness to stay focused and engaged with others until the final hours.

How fitting that her last word spoken was "Amen" after a prayer led by her pastor.

During one of our planning sessions, Sandra made one last request regarding her funeral. She wanted to address those who attended her celebration of life with a personal message. Little did she know that 950 people would go through the receiving line the evening before. The church would be at full capacity, with an adjacent facility set up with sound and video piped in. As you learn more about Sandra, you will understand why there was such an outpouring. Here is the quote from Sandra that I read verbatim to the attendees:

"Thank you for taking time from your daily routine and busy schedules to celebrate my life here on earth. May you always walk in sunshine, may your heart be filled with joy, and may God be with you until we meet again. Love, Sandra."

I hope you enjoy reading about Sandra's and my journey through life. The stories are real, and the people are real. The names and places are exact as best I can remember. I did not sugarcoat the facts or make them better or worse to add interest. I have added afterthoughts in *italics* at the end of each memory, which may be of interest or offer further explanation of events.

And to Sandra, my friend then, now, and forever: thanks for the memories.

So That's How We Won the War!

O h, sweet summertime—the creator of beautiful memories! With summer comes freedom to roam the outdoors, linger outside until darkness settles playing tag and hide-and-seek and catching lightning bugs. We shed our heavy winter clothes for lighter and more comfortable apparel, including our shoes. Winters for Sandra and me were cold and harsh. We both lived in houses heated with a central coal or wood stove, although we did eventually graduate to an oil stove, providing warmer heat with less chance of getting burned when bumping into the unit. Living was mainly confined to the kitchen as it was always warm until the last meal was prepared and the cooking stove cooled, but reading, TV (when we finally got one), baths, and dressing took place around the coal or wood stove.

Washing off, referred to as a sponge bath by the elderly, then quickly dressing while trying to maintain your dignity was a challenge in the winter. Subsequently, one must make a mad dash to jump into a bed piled high with quilts, warm a spot, and remain in that position until morning.

But as the days grew longer and the gray skies grew brighter, the sun produced enough power for trees to sprout fresh leaves, dogwoods to bloom, and daylilies to blossom with bright yellow buds. People smiled more often, moved a little faster, and in general developed an overall pleasant demeanor. I looked forward to coming home from school on the day Grandma would replace the red velvet drapes that drearily dressed the windows over the winter, shielding the warmth inside from the wind, with freshly starched Priscilla curtains. The heavy quilts were removed from the beds, hung on the clothesline to air, and then packed away and replaced by newly washed, air-dried seersucker bedspreads and white starched sheets. Oh, we loved summer!

As young children, just shy of being assigned chores, our most significant challenge was to play without getting in the way of busy adults. And play we did! Our lack of material things failed to slow us down and only drove us to develop a strong "pretend" game through our creative powers. So each morning we rose, ate, dressed, and then met in the field separating our homes. Scattered about were sheds, old garages, and poorly built structures perfect for playhouses, simulated downtowns, schools, and such. But our favorite pretend activity was playing church.

Now, I need to lay some groundwork for you. Sandra's parents were quite religious and attended an independent Baptist church—not one of the organized, larger churches that belonged to a prestigious conference. I mentioned earlier that my grandfather was a Pentecostal Holiness preacher and an excellent one, I might add. He could be heard over the loudest crying baby, the out-of-tune organ, and a streaming chorus of amens from the congregation. Altar calls were his specialty. Members had three chances a week to participate in an altar call—Sunday morning, Sunday evening, and Wednesday night prayer meeting—before receiving a home visit from Preacher Robinson to determine if someone had backslid.

Two services on Sunday, prayer meetings on Wednesday, holding revivals several times a year, calling on shut-ins, and visiting the sick in the hospital will keep a preacher quite busy. But preaching did not always pay so well. If the collection plate was not full, as was often the case, the church bills were paid, contributions to missionary work came second, it seems there was always a building fund, and my grandfather would take only what was left. Consequently, many preachers had second jobs. So did Grandpa: he became a Knapp Shoe salesman.

I'm sure only a few readers have heard of the Knapp Shoe Company; much less familiar with their weary salesmen. But I was proud of Grandpa. He carried a large suitcase with the name Knapp Shoes stenciled on the outside. Inside were shoe samples made from real leather, flyers with pictures of more shoes, all the colors available, order forms, and an actual sizing apparatus with a sliding contraption to measure length and width. Sandra and I measured every obliging foot in the neighborhood and eventually became quite adept at using this contraption.

Thinking back, Grandpa must have been an early entrepreneur (although I'm sure I never heard him use that word). I believe this because Grandpa, to further his second career, purchased a small, brown tent on which he had stenciled KNAPP SHOES on the scalloped front flap. At times (between services) he would load all this paraphernalia in his 1935 DeSoto with running boards on the side, pitch his tent by the roadside or, with permission, in someone's front yard, and set about taking orders. I never accompanied him on these trips, but his return was always exciting. Grandma would either make a clucking sound with her tongue or join him at the kitchen table to sort the orders, count the money, and send information to the company. A few weeks later, the shoes would arrive, and Grandpa would make his delivery rounds. I assume Grandma's mood depended on the number of orders in hand.

The only reason you need to know all this is the tent. When not in use, the tent was set up in our front yard. That's correct—the front yard, not the back. Developments with HOA rules had not made their way to our small town. When not in use, the Knapp Shoe tent became Sandra's and my church.

We gathered logs to set up pews, fashioned a pulpit from an old wooden box, and two concrete blocks with a slab of lumber from the woodshed served as our altar. We ushered in all the young kids (who were also challenged to stay out of the way of adults) in the neighborhood to sit among the dolls that completed our faithful congregation. We had plenty of songbooks, and we did love to sing! Until Sandra died and as long as I live, Southern gospel music will always be in our souls.

We saved, sanctified, and brought the Holy Spirit to everyone who entered our makeshift house of worship. We buried every animal that died in the neighborhood (hopefully none that didn't). We prayed for people we were convinced had sinned and were stumbling down the wrong path. We weren't sure what adultery was, but after hearing the adults speak of Mr. Hewitt committing it, we prayed for him too. He evidently was healed because he lived to be in his eighties.

Notice I mentioned we only involved kids our age or younger. I had a sister four years my junior, too young to attend our services or be entrusted to our care. Sandra at that time was the youngest in her family, but we both had older brothers who paid little attention to us except to satisfy a need to aggravate and belittle us and make our life miserable. So they were banished from our tent.

We never grew tired of playing church and patterned our services after my grandfather's church and Sandra's Baptist church. Our passion and loyalty to prayer paid off significantly a few years later for both us and, more importantly, our country.

Around noon each day, Grandma would call us in for lunch. Lunch would be waiting on the white and black porcelain table where we sat quietly as Grandma listened intently to the radio. The ivory colored plastic Philco resided on top of a small refrigerator. Tuning was an art. The radio knob must be turned at a particular angle, and the tuner moved very slowly. Once the station came in clear, one's hand must be jerked away quickly, making sure not to disturb the dial. At noon, the news came on, and this was a critical time for communication in our country.

Sandra and I were referred to as war babies, as was everyone born during World War II, but we did not know what a war was or how terrified our parents and grandparents were during this time. Our country was involved in the Korean conflict, and having just recovered from World War II, all ears were once again glued to the radio. We made an effort to listen, but little became clear to us except the announcer sounded truly serious. Sometimes he would deepen his voice, and my grandmother would start praying.

We needed to find out exactly what this "war" thing meant. So we asked my brother, Jimmy, who explained in one brief sentence. "Well," he said, "we are fighting with Korea, and if we win, we get to bomb them, and if they win, they get to bomb us."

We knew what a bomb was, as people were still talking about Hiroshima, so we certainly hoped we would win. *Surely*, we thought, *we are bigger and braver, with a monster bomb, so no worries.* Still, the nagging fear would not go away.

A few days later, as we played with our dolls and tea sets in the front yard, we suddenly heard a thunderous roar. We looked up, and the western sky was darkened with huge, bulky green planes. They flew in formation with giant propellers whirling—much lower than planes normally fly when taking passengers to exotic locations. My brother, red-faced and wide-eyed, ran from the house, slamming the front door and screaming, "We lost, we lost! They are coming to bomb us!"

We were terrified. Of course, we didn't know the difference between a cargo plane and a B-52 bomber, nor did we know Fort Bragg, the largest Army base in the country, was less than two hundred miles away, but we weren't taking any chances. We rushed to our tent, fell before the makeshift altar, and began praying. We admitted to every fault and begged forgiveness for every fib and shortcoming. We prayed for our lives, for the lives of everyone around us, and for Jack (that was Grandpa's dog, who had chewed Grandma's apron that morning), and we didn't stop praying until the skies were clear and silent. Were they going to bomb a larger town? Had something deterred them? Or had we prayed with such fervor that our prayers were answered? We chose the latter.

A few days later as we assembled at Grandma's table for lunch, an exuberant newscaster announced an armistice had been signed, and the Korean conflict was over. Our troops would be returning home! Grandma bowed her head and whispered, "Thank you, Jesus."

Sandra and I looked at each other, smiled, and wondered silently, Would the world ever know about those two little girls in a small town in North Carolina who prayed us through that terrible time and helped bring an end to the *war*?

Thanks for the memory, Sandra.

Postscript: Grandpa had his first stroke driving back from one of his Knapp Shoe trips. It was minor, and he went on to pastor a church in North Wilkesboro before another debilitating disease forced him to retire. People who wore Knapp shoes were extraordinarily loyal, and those lucky enough to have owned a pair still swear nothing comes close to a pair of Knapp shoes.

In a Pickle

S andra's mother was a prolific canner. At the first hint of spring, aided by the Farmer's Almanac, her father began tilling the large field separating our homes and readying the earth for planting. As vegetables ripened, the canning started in earnest, and by fall, the storage shelves in the room adjacent to the back porch would be filled with fresh vegetables for the winter months.

We cared little about the green beans, squash or other good-for-you vegetables, but those pickles were a different story. It started one day when we walked into Sandra's kitchen famished from a busy morning playing in our playhouse. On this already hot summer day, the kitchen was unbearable as steam rose from the large pots on the stove sterilizing canning jars. It was past noon, and we were hot and hungry. Wholly occupied with her canning, Mrs. Hass ordered us to get a jar of her pickles from the storage room off the back porch, go outside, and eat them under the tree.

Pickles were not our first choice for lunch, but without an option, we did as we were told and retreated to the white Adirondack chairs under the large shade tree on the side yard where we opened our first jar of pickles. Sandra turned on the hosepipe just enough to produce a small trickle, pulled it close by so we could instantly wash away the bad taste we were expecting. We were pleasantly surprised at the sweet tasting pickles. By the time we finished the jar, we had developed a serious craving for Mrs. Hass's canned pickles and drinking from the hosepipe. *(Note: A hosepipe is just a garden hose, but for some reason, it was always called a hosepipe in our town. I still refer to it as such.)*

One would think parents were pleased we had developed a craving for something other than a Fifth Avenue bar but our second trip to duplicate our ritual under the tree was met with consternation. "*No*, you girls cannot just go to the canning room and eat all the pickles! The canning has to last us all winter," and so on and so on, repeated Mrs. Hass.

But the craving would not go away, so as the shelves became packed with pickles (we left everything else alone), we learned to reach behind to the second row, pull out a jar, and slide the others forward, thereby hiding our sin. This ritual became a standard procedure for us as we perfected our playhouse in the dilapidated garage behind my house.

By this time, my grandparents had moved to North Wilkesboro—about an hour away in a '35 DeSoto but a lot closer now—to pastor a church. My family had since moved across the street on the corner. Behind our mill-type house was a good-sized garage with three rooms. I guess the entrance to the road would house a car (if we had one), but our space was used for storage. There was a loft and two other rooms sectioned off for different needs. The area we chose to construct our playhouse had once served as a chicken coop.

Lack of store-bought toys forced us to move in a different direction, depending greatly on our creative powers, so we took this playhouse construction seriously. We considered it "our house," and we fully intended to build it so we could live there. There were many artifacts (more like junk) stored in this section; we utilized them if possible or just moved them to the corner. We carefully sectioned off rooms by bringing in lumber rescued from destruction around the neighborhood; we constructed other furniture from bricks and old buckets or pails. We even had curtains fashioned from the discarded material we discovered in the loft over the garage area.

Our most prized decorating achievement, however, was the couch we constructed from three broken ladder-back chairs we saved from C. J. Shook's fire.

Mr. Shook lived alone across the street in a strange two-room house. The rooms were separate but connected in the middle by an open area. The roof covered the entire house, but the area in the middle was not enclosed. This was where Mr. Shook stored his wood and other items he accumulated or items that just showed up from time to time.

I don't think I ever heard Mr. Shook speak a word. He would leave for work, come home, chop wood, piddle with his tools, or remain inside. He was always clad in overalls and seldom had visitors, and we never saw the inside his house. We knew the room on the left was a kitchen because smoke came from the chimney, and this was where he stayed most of the time. At night, he would exit from the kitchen door, walk to the other end of the structure, and enter what we assumed was the bedroom door.

He seemed to be a good person—just preferred his privacy. However, about once a month he would build a fire behind his house and burn items stored in the open area. People would drop off items for him to burn (no burning permits necessary), so I guess he was performing a service for the community—or perhaps he was an early environmentalist.

Sandra and I watched one evening as he prepared a bonfire when we noticed three old ladder-back chairs in the burn pile. They looked a little lopsided, with some rungs missing and a few ladders broken, but for playhouse purposes, they might as well have been on display in the window of the Newton furniture store downtown on the square.

We raced across the street, not totally fearless, as we had never had an encounter with Mr. Shook, but quickly asked if we could have the three chairs. Without looking up and still not speaking, he nodded yes. It took three trips, but finally the chairs were safely stored in our "living room." By the next day, the chairs had been bound together with old potholder strings found in the loft; several old pillows made for a nice seat cushion, and we even surmised that this newly fashioned loveseat was suitable for a nap if necessary.

So we continued to work and improve our playhouse. We swept the dirt floors, washed the broken dishes, and even picked wildflowers for our Mason jar vases. The rooms, sectioned off by lumber, were clearly defined. Our dolls were our children, which we religiously fed, bathed, dressed, schooled, and put to bed. Our husbands, selected from movie star books, changed often but hastened to glamorous jobs each morning. We ate lunch or any meal we could in our house and from time to time entertained guests. We never did feel the need to explain why we all lived together in one house, for explanations were not necessary in our pretend life.

Summer gave way to fall, the days shortened, and the air became chillier, infringing significantly on our playhouse time. One day we were happily playing house but continued to be bothered by the cold. Our eyes wandered to the artifact/junk corner where we spotted a rusted potbellied stove. It hit us at the same time: *We'll simply build a fire!*

It took some effort and time to pull the heavy cast iron stove to the middle of the room. We had seen many fires built in such stoves, so we knew the routine. Paper was essential. First, you wadded up the paper and stuffed it into the belly of the stove. Then you added a few sticks. No problem finding paper. People kept stacks of paper just for this purpose, so we pilfered enough to meet our needs. Sticks for kindling were gathered from the yard, so all we needed now were matches.

Matches were a staple in every kitchen. Both of ours featured a large box of striking wood matches in a hanging matchbox holder of tin decorated with red flowers. Outside we could see Sandra's mother moving around in her kitchen. My mother could not be seen but most likely was also in the kitchen. While we debated what to do, my mother suddenly yelled (everybody yelled back then) that she was walking across the street to Dessie's house and for us to stay in the yard. *"Okay,"* we answered, trying to keep our excitement to a minimum.

Once clear, we sneaked into the kitchen and picked a handful of matches from my mother's tin box. We closed the playhouse door tightly, peeked through the windows to be sure no one was near, and then pulled the tattered curtains closed. I'm not sure who struck the first match, but it was harder than we anticipated. Some broke in half, and others refused to flame. Finally only one match was left. Fortunately, Sandra remembered that her father always struck the match on the stove, held it to the paper until it caught fire, dropped the match and paper into the stove, and then quickly slid the top over the opening. It worked! However, our happiness was brief and followed by sheer terror.

Immediately flames rose from the round hole on the back of the stove. The hole was intended to be connected to the flue, which must be vented outside (as we later learned). *Holy cow!* We were horrified. It made sense to cover the hole where fire and smoke were leaping which we did with a plank, but then blinding smoke began filling the room. "Water," Sandra yelled, "we have to put it out with water!" But the hosepipe was at the front of the house and would not reach. "The pickles! Grab the pickles!"

Our pilfered pickles were well hidden in a box in the artifact corner. Blindly groping through the heavy smoke, we finally located the pickles. We grabbed as many as we could carry, quickly screwed off the tops and started pouring the pickles and juice in the fire. It took our whole stash to extinguish the fire, but the smoke lingered, and the stench became unbearable.

Staggering outside, sick and nauseated from the smell of smoke mingled with burnt pickles and pickle juice, we aimlessly wandered across the street toward Dessie's house, where she and my mother were sitting on the front porch. The offensive odor was still clinging to us, but we were too sick and scared to notice until my mother asked, "Have you girls been playing with fire?"

We recovered quickly. "No," we replied, "that's just C. J. Shook burning trash again." That seemed to satisfy them.

Thanks for the memory, Sandra.

Postscript: We had many great times in that old garage. A large apple tree grew on one side, providing access to the tin roof that offered a clear view of the neighborhood. I was and still am afraid of heights, but Sandra would encourage me to keep going until we reached the top. Maybe in a later chapter, I will have the courage to share a scene we observed one day through a neighbor's window.

Hollywood or Bust

We must have been around nine or ten years of age when our obsession with movie stars began. Fueling this preoccupation were three very pretty teenage sisters who lived across the street. We adored them. They wore makeup, short shorts, and cotton blouses unbuttoned except for the three top buttons, allowing the two loose sides to be tied in a casual knot under their precisely pointed bosoms, made possible by the popular circular stitched bras of that era. Every day from noon to one the sisters lay in the sun, never sweating or turning red, just a lovely shade of brown; we thought they looked like Italians! The pronounced yet natural swinging of their hips came from carefully studying the walk of glamorous actresses plus hours of practice in front of the mirror to develop a sophisticated walk without sashaying promiscuously. Even their names rang of intrigue—Jonell, Rozell, and Maybel. Sandra and I decided that when we came of age, we would change our names to create the same effect—to something like Trixie and Roxie.

Most afternoons, after household chores and when tanning and primping were completed, the sisters would settle down on a quilt spread in the backyard under a huge shade tree surrounded by movie star books. While Sandra and I spent any loose change on Pepsi Colas, the sisters hurried to the drugstore monthly to purchase the latest editions of *Photoplay*, *Movie Stars*, *Movie Classics*, and other stardom magazines. They inspected the pictures carefully and read the articles aloud, followed by a barrage of opinions and predictions. Sandra and I listened carefully and then re-discussed between ourselves.

19

We became well versed on the marriages, divorces, children, and who was involved with whom, most of which was gossip but to us was factual and indeed more interesting than any news Edward R. Murrow delivered nightly over the small Airline TV with rabbit-ears.

We studied the pictures (all carefully touched up and airbrushed) and noticed that the sisters had perfected the same looks: arched eyebrows, blue eye shadow, lip shapes and shades, winged eyeliner, and rouge. Their dresser was full of Revlon, Maybelline, Max Factor, Helena Rubinstein, Lady Ester powder, Evening in Paris perfume, and Pond's Cold Cream. Once a picture of Lana Turner with a pink neck scarf and green front-button sweater appeared in a magazine. The next day the sisters wore green sweaters and pink scarves with their shorts, even though it was August.

What I remember most about the "ells," as we came to refer to them, was their kindness. We were two scrawny kids nipping at their heels, asking questions, and just generally getting in the way. Yet I can't remember an unkind word or even a sign of impatience. So we aspired to follow their lead and likewise studied the Hollywood scene carefully.

We had no idea where Hollywood might be; I barely remembered moving from Virginia, and Sandra had been born in this town. The world as we knew it consisted of our neighborhood and the immediately surrounding area. For sure, there was more outside the city limits, but with no concept of distance, we assumed Hollywood was around some curve or over a hill.

Besides, one afternoon as we were sitting on my front porch, we convinced ourselves that Janet Leigh and Tony Curtis had passed by in a new convertible. It was a fine car, one we had not seen before, with a license tag of a different color. She wore a Hawaiian print scarf on her head to protect her stylish "updo" from the wind, but his black wavy hair was so perfect it appeared the wind was gently combing through his locks. Where they were going was a mystery, as the road ran into Two Joe Hill, which was a stomach-churning roller-coaster ride we frequently enjoyed on our bikes. A shortcut? Perhaps to Hollywood? Or on their way to make a movie!

Another time, Sandra was confident she had spied Robert Mitchum having his hair cut at the North Newton barber shop. We hoped the barber was competent and protected Robert's carefully arched, hair-tonic-laden wave on top—his trademark.

So these fantasies grew, and we added making movies and playing movie star to our pretend collection. And then, one Sunday afternoon, hope sprang into reality.

In those days, if a family had a car, there was only one. The time had not yet arrived when cars were standard for every household. City buses were always full, taxis as well, and of course as kids, we just walked or rode our bikes if we needed to go somewhere. For families who did have cars, the Sunday afternoon drive was a ritual, and Sandra's dad owned a car. So on this particular Sunday afternoon, the family filled the car, rolled down the windows so air could circulate, and went for a drive. Returning an hour or so later, Sandra bolted from the vehicle and with unrestrained excitement ran directly to my house.

Between gasps she managed to blurt, "I know where Hollywood is!" I just looked at her, surprised but hopeful I had not misunderstood. She loudly repeated, "I know where Hollywood is!"

Finally she caught her breath, sat down on the front steps, and began to explain. The Sunday drive had taken them beyond the city limits, and with the window down (no air conditioned cars yet) she began for the first time to absorb everything she saw. At first there were just houses, some farms, horses, and churches, but then the homes seemed larger. One even had a pond out front. Then she spotted a small mountain or a large hill! Her excitement grew. We knew the Hollywood sign was on a slope, so Sandra became suspicious that perhaps she was near the back side of Hollywood. There was a sign beside a road that led up the big hill, and beside it was a beautiful home almost identical to a photo in one of the "ells'" movie magazines.

Sandra tried to read the sign, but it passed too quickly. There were more nice homes perched atop hills on both sides. She hoped her father would turn toward the mountain, which for sure would lead to the town, but instead he circled back in the opposite direction. Still, she was convinced she had found Hollywood—it just had to be—*and* was sure she could find her way again. We just had to go!

For an excursion this important, we needed to plan carefully as it would probably take us all day. Monday was washday, so by Tuesday our Sunday dresses would be freshly starched and ironed. That gave us time to polish our black patent leather shoes with Vaseline and gather our food supply. Wednesday became the designated day, so Wednesday morning we rose as soon as the whistle blew for the first shift at the furniture factory and put on our freshly finished Sunday dresses and shiny black patent leather shoes with white, lace-trimmed socks. (We fully expected to encounter several movie stars and wanted to look our best.) We each filled a Mason jar with Kool-Aid and prepared two tomato sandwiches each, carefully wrapped in wax paper. After placing our goods in the old wire handlebar baskets on our rusted bikes, with unbridled enthusiasm, coupled with sheer determination, we set out for Hollywood.

It was hot, sweltering hot. We made it to the overhead bridge. *(To this day I have no idea why they called it the overhead bridge. The bridge crossed over the railroad tracks and rose slightly to provide clearance for the trains. There are many duplicates around which are just called bridges. But ours was the overhead bridge.)* Distance wise, my best guess is the overhead bridge was about three-quarters of a mile from where we started this adventure. We drank about half of our Kool-Aid, ate one tomato sandwich, and rested for quite some time. Sandra was still confident. We need to make it to the courthouse downtown, she insisted, as that was where they turned on Sunday.

Sometime later, we collapsed on the courthouse square where we quickly guzzled the remainder of our Kool-Aid and inhaled our last tomato sandwich. When finally we felt some energy restored in our bodies, we stood up, mounted our bikes, and considered our options. Sandra looked around but disguised her confusion well. "I think it's that way," she said and pointed to our right. Of course it wasn't, but we rode off unknowingly and soon found ourselves on a busy highway across from a baseball field with a sign that read AMERICAN LEGION STADIUM.

We had heard of this stadium. There was a rumor that the yearly carnival in conjunction with the Old Soldiers' Reunion planned on relocating to this stadium, rather than a site in North Newton beside the overhead bridge, within walking distance of our homes. We must be far from home, we thought, and now entirely lost.

It was getting hotter, and without liquids, we were suffering from exhaustion and dehydration. Slowly we retraced our steps by identifying familiar landmarks, until finally we arrived at the square downtown. What a relief! Inspired by this achievement, our pace quickened as we hastened to a local department store where a public water fountain was available.

However, within minutes we were overcome with fear. The town was deserted. Banks, offices, stores—all were closed. We had totally forgotten it was Wednesday! It may seem strange today as we are accustomed to extended mall hours and twenty-four-hour grocery stores, but this was a much more laid back time. It was the norm for stores on Wednesday afternoon to simply close down. The factories and some offices stayed open, but businesses located downtown (as most were) just closed their doors. *(The best explanation I have heard for this custom is that it prevented the store owners and employees from working a full six-day week as it was imperative for businesses to be operational on Saturdays, when farmers came to town. If they all closed at the same time, the competition would be neutralized.)*

Without a choice, we trudged along, thirsty and hungry. When we caught sight of the overhead bridge, we knew we were closing in on home. Thankfully, it was a little cooler, but with our energy level so low, we were forced to push rather than ride our bikes.

Exhausted, dusty, soaked with sweat, hair drenched, shoes and socks long since removed, we rounded the curve to my house. We were two disheveled, dirty little girls pushing bikes with empty Mason jars rattling in the wire handlebar baskets, and the first thing we saw was my mother sitting in her green metal porch chair with her arms crossed. We both knew what that meant.

We spotted her from a distance, and any energy we still had evaporated and was replaced by fear and dread. As we entered the yard, my mother rose from her chair, hands now on her hips, and came down the steps to meet us. *"And just where have you girls been all day?"*

I was almost in tears, but Sandra, not quite ready to admit defeat, reminded me of Rita Hayworth as she proudly threw her head back, flipped her naturally curly hair, walked past my mother, and clearly, with dignity and confidence, replied, *"Hollywood!"* My mother looked stunned as Sandra kept walking and pushing her bike straight to her house.

Thanks for the memory, Sandra.

Postscript: We later realized the Hollywood hill was actually Little Mountain. It is little, for a mountain, but its real purpose was to house a fire tower; hence the road winding up the hill. Later we learned from experience that the road was used quite frequently as a lover's lane. Some lovely homes surrounded the mountain, including one with a pond out front. One beside the road also housed a business, making it seem larger. You must remember, however, that our comparison of beautiful homes at that time was mainly limited to mill houses and quick builds by landlords.

The three sisters have now passed away. However, Mabel actually was Sandra's neighbor for a time and attended her funeral. All three maintained their good looks and were beautiful women throughout their lives.

Sally, Fannie, and Junior

As adults, Sandra and I often reflected on the amount of freedom we enjoyed growing up and ultimately concluded we had essentially raised ourselves. For the most part, I was reared by a single parent who somehow managed to feed and clothe us on a waitress's salary. Wives who stayed home were kept extremely busy with *all* the cleaning, cooking, gardening, laundry, freezing, canning, and yard work, leaving little time for formal child-rearing.

Day care facilities were slowly finding their way into communities, but as a youngster, I only remember one during my childhood years in our town, and it stayed that way until churches became involved. Consequently, the entire neighborhood assumed the right to watch over, discipline, correct, and feed children who misbehaved, got hungry, or wandered too far off the beaten path.

We knew everyone within blocks of our home and thought nothing of dropping in when lunch was ready in hopes of receiving an invite to join them. That was how we met Crazy Sally—a title she had been given by the neighborhood.

On a dirt road which ran beside Sandra's home stood a dilapidated, red-shingled house. Sally lived there with her mother. As I recall, it had four rooms and a small bathroom built on the back porch. Sally rose early each morning and immediately ran outside where she would sweep the dirt yard with the same broom used on the linoleum floors inside, trim the little patches of grass with scissors, and resolutely pull weeds from her garden.

Sally was obsessed with weeds invading her garden. She would stand at the top of the rows, staring intently as she waited for a weed to pop up. We watched with her at first, hoping to be helpful, with her continually asking, "Do you see anything yet?"

When she wasn't performing her outside ritual, Sally was flitting about the house in the same hurried manner, busy as a bee but accomplishing little. She was an excellent cook who kept a pot of water boiling on the stove all day. Once we asked why water bubbled continuously. She explained, seeming surprised we did not know, that the water was in case she needed to cook something that required boiling water. It would always be ready, and she would not have to wait for the water to boil. It made perfect sense to us; it seemed our mothers were frequently waiting for water to boil before starting dinner.

Sally also wore the same dress for a week. On Saturday, she slipped into a tattered but fresh, cleaned and ironed dress which she would wear for the next seven days. Her ritual began early Saturday with a good bath, hair washed and wound on paper bag strips for curling, and topped off with clean clothes. These were not Sunday clothes, mind you, as Sally did not attend church.

We observed Sally's many eccentric activities while traveling the dirt road past her house, which also led to the creek path. The road was a dead end for cars, but the children in the neighborhood had formed a path to the creek. We spent many days dangling our feet in the water, catching tadpoles, building dams, or just wading in the creek to keep cool. Sandra and I used only one small section because the central part of the creek, which was a little deeper with a steeper hill, was the property of the older boys in the neighborhood who made it clear that no girls were allowed.

One day, as we were heading toward the creek, we saw Sally on her knees, peering under the rotting front porch, encouraging "Butchy" to come out and play. Assuming Sally had acquired a dog, we eagerly ran to help. Sally was poking her broom toward the object, urging Butchy to please come out. Overcome with sympathy for poor Sally, who had lost her dog, Sandra and I quickly fell to our knees to help. Then we screamed and ran full speed toward the creek.

Sally had cornered the largest rat we had ever cast eyes on, and it had the misfortune of being misidentified as a dog and affectionately named and claimed by Sally. Most frightening to us was that Butchy appeared to have had enough of Sally and with bared teeth was ready to pounce. We reached the creek in record time.

After a fun-filled day at the creek, we carefully walked past Sally's house on the way home, but no one was in sight. Several days later, we casually asked about Butchy, but Sally had no recollection of the incident.

We enjoyed bantering back and forth with Sally, sometimes snickering at her antics, but to us, she was amusing and harmless, plus she seemed to look forward to our visits. As I mentioned before, Sally was an excellent cook, and we could depend on her to have food prepared throughout the day.

But our main attraction to Sally was her stories. After supper, in the late afternoon, Sally tended to wear out. Finishing the supper dishes, she would settle into a shabby rocking chair on the porch with a glass of sweet tea. The ladies in the neighborhood did not visit with Sally, but this did not keep her from carrying on lengthy conversations with people who did not exist. We found this interesting enough that one evening we took a seat on the front porch steps and became enthralled with Sally's tales.

In vividly descriptive language, Sally began sharing with us her experiences as a debutante. She engaged our interest by describing her gorgeous gowns made of flowing taffeta, sometimes with a netted shoulder wrap, dazzling diamonds adorning her ears and ruby necklaces so heavy her back still hurt to this day. Sally spoke of dancing in large ballrooms with live orchestras and being delivered home in long limousines. Her many beaus stood in line for dances, and she had trouble selecting from the bunch, as they were all so handsome.

The lavish parties took her around the world, but she could not remember the names of places or how she got there. She stared hypnotically at the sky when she spoke of these events and seemed almost sane as she captured our imagination and took us along on her journey. Sometimes she would hum tunes, which we never recognized.

But Sally had another problem which resulted in our being banned from these visits. It seems that every Saturday night after dark and until the wee hours of the morning, Sally was frequented by many male visitors who stayed for a short period and left, followed by others who would enter or wait on the porch. We saw nothing wrong with Sally having visitors—she was quite lonely during the week—but our mothers were aghast, and we were forbidden to enter the house again. We could only speak to Sally when she was outside.

Sally did not seem to notice when our visits became infrequent. Soon afterward, we learned from the neighborhood gossips that Sally had been taken to Morganton, the home of Broughton Hospital, an asylum for the mentally ill. Morganton is a picture-perfect town in the North Carolina foothills, but unfortunately, when someone said they were going to Morganton, people just assumed it was so they could be admitted to Broughton.

I don't know what happened to Sally's mother. She slept most of the time; perhaps she was ill, but the red house finally fell apart and was torn down along with Sally's dreams.

Fannie and Junior

I do not recall how or exactly when Fannie entered our lives. She worked in the mill. (We had several mills, and though we might say "the mill on Davis" or "the mill on College Street," they were all referred to as "the mill.") At one time she rented a room close to the mill but later leased a two-room house a couple of blocks from us, so I'm guessing she just started visiting around the neighborhood.

Fannie was harmless and always held a steady job, but now I can see how she struggled to handle things on her own and often set herself up to be exploited. She seemed to be two people. Fannie would come to our house, bring cookies, sit and talk, and then go home. We would hear later she had told people we stole her cookies.

One weekend, she volunteered to take Sandra and me to the movies. The invitation was *huge* for us. Fannie did not have a car, so we were to meet her at the corner intersection. We would walk to North Newton, eat at the Central Café, and afterward walk to the movies downtown. We were standing on the corner at least thirty minutes early. As planned, we had lunch, went to the movies (where she bought us drinks and popcorn), stopped again at the Central Café for ice cream, and started home.

That was when Fannie's persona number two emerged. Suddenly, her demeanor changed dramatically, her pace quickened, and we were challenged to keep up. Her face became flushed, and she began spewing vicious accusations over and over. She shouted that she could not do this anymore. Did we think she was made of money? How was she going to feed herself in the coming weeks or pay her rent?

Her yelling was relentless until we reached the corner. Then persona number one returned and asked if we'd had a good time, and would we like to go to the movies again? Lamely, we nodded yes.

That's how it went with Fannie. Everyone just understood her challenges, but she was a good citizen, and she worked. Working, we learned, was significant. But you can see how it was possible for Fannie to be outwitted by others, which happened often.

Our most notorious encounter with Fannie came later. Fannie was an accepted part of the neighborhood, though sometimes weeks might pass without her presence. Later, she would reappear without explanation. It is essential to understand that Fannie was a grown woman with the same desires as other full-blooded females but without the ability to manage these urges.

On the other side of the tracks (we were on the right side of the river but still on the wrong side of the tracks) lived Junior, a man about Fannie's age and of the same mental ability. Junior rode his bicycle all over town, through every neighborhood. He was just there, and nobody ever questioned his goings and comings. At some point, fortunately or not, his and Fannie's paths crossed.

Neither knew how to court or how to date. We would see Junior riding his bike all over the neighborhood trying to find Fannie or wait for her to come home. If he found Fannie number one, they would sit on the sidewalk or someone's front porch talking. If it was Fannie number two, an argument broke out, and Junior pedaled away frantically.

I am not sure what happened to Fannie's rental home during this time, but for some reason, perhaps failure to pay the rent, she no longer occupied the dwelling. She was renting a room from someone on a parallel street but roamed the neighborhood, especially on weekends. She was often invited in if dinner was ready, or sometimes, if no one was home, Fannie would be sitting on the couch when family members returned home.

This happened at my house one Friday night. My mother and younger sister, Judy, were at the neighbors participating in a long-standing tradition in the South, the weekly Friday night fish fry.

Sandra was spending the night with me, and after watching TV, we retired to the bedroom I shared with my sister. Suddenly we heard the slam of the front door and voices in the living room. The living room and front porch lights were on as instructed for safety reasons and to aid my mother and sister when returning home in the dark. My bedroom light was off.

We listened to voices entering the hallway but could not identify the intruders, so we assumed the worst and immediately hid under the bed. Two people kept talking, and finally we recognized them as Fannie and Junior, but they were not making sense. Having determined no one was home, they still felt compelled to get away from the light. That was when they entered my room, where the talk turned to whether they should use the bed or go behind the door to perform this "act."

Holy cow! *The Act!* Could it possibly be? We had so many questions about this "act," and now we had a front-row seat. With hand signals, we told each other to be quiet. There seemed to be a lot of commotion, rustling of clothes, and shuffling of feet. She muttered that she couldn't get comfortable; he replied that they had to stay behind the door. *Why?* we wondered. *They don't know we're here. Just crack it a little, please!*

They banged into the walls and doors and finally fell to the floor—when suddenly, without warning, Fannie number two emerged, screaming they had to leave. Why was he doing this to her? He was just like everybody else! She shoved him backward so forcefully that he hit the dresser, tumbled over a stool, and landed on the floor within a foot of where we lay staring wide-eyed.

Fortunately, it was too dark for Junior to make out the two girls frozen in awestruck terror. After much scurrying, we heard the front door slam, and they were gone.

We glared at each other for a long time before bursting into uncontrollable laughter. Some young people learn about the facts of life from books, parents, or teachers or in other proper ways. But Sandra and I, wouldn't you know, it just had to be Fannie and Junior.

Thanks for the memory, Sandra.

Postscript: *I don't know what happened to Fannie, Junior, or Sally. I suppose today special provisions would be made for them or maybe a lifetime of institutionalization. Would they have been better off? I doubt it, but perhaps they would have been safer. They were relatively harmless and well tolerated by the community. Maybe limited freedom and a glimpse of real life are better than none.*

TV and Joining the Circus

There were only eight houses on the large block and dead-end street where Sandra and I spent our early elementary school years, including two homes on the corner facing an intersecting street. At one time, eleven kids near our age, with a few teenagers thrown into the mix, called it home. Our street continually bustled with children from hardworking families who were left to fends for themselves most of the day.

One house on the block, however, was occupied by a childless husband and wife. It was a small, white four-room house with green shutters. The owner painted the house religiously every two years early in Fourth-of-July week, when the local mills shut down. The second part of the week, the couple made their annual trek to Myrtle Beach. The wife worked in the garden every afternoon and spent at least half of Saturday tending her flowers and vegetables. The house was impeccably maintained, and the yard expertly manicured. If my memory serves me correctly, their last name was Sigmon.

Not that any of us cared how often the house was painted or how well the grounds were kept. We cared mainly that it was the only house on the block with a TV! It took a while for TVs to make their way into homes across America and even longer to find their way to our neighborhood. This was the only TV in the immediate vicinity, and without children in the household for us to befriend and gain an invitation to watch this device, we had to depend on our creativity. Even at this early age, we observed and later confirmed in life, people without children seem to have more things and more time and were better off financially.

We were not entirely ignorant of TV. The furniture and appliance stores downtown kept sets in their windows to lure customers inside. Western Auto was the favorite. The store kept the TV going from opening to closing, and there was speculation that a full-time person was situated on the roof to adjust the antennae when needed—which was all the time.

As a side note, Western Auto was also our favorite venue at Christmastime. This otherwise boring auto parts store would turn an entire section into a magnificent display of toys. Samples of toy pedal cars, sporty tricycles, real-life dolls, and washing machine replicas filled the windows. When we returned to school after the Christmas holidays, the teachers had the custom of allowing each student to stand in front of the room and announce what they had received for Christmas. If one was lucky enough, as some in South Newton were, to obtain a toy from Western Auto, a tagline would be added, such as "I got a blond, curly-haired doll from Western Auto." Of course, those of us in North Newton often added the same tagline despite the fact these toys were out of budget for our Santa Claus.

People would gather in groups at the windows of these various retailers to watch the TV picture devoid of sound. There were only three main channels, all located in Charlotte, representing the three leading networks, CBS, ABC, and NBC. A few of our friends from school had TVs, and we were sometimes invited to their homes after the bell rang to watch our favorite Westerns which aired at five thirty weekdays—*Hopalong Cassidy, Red Ryder, Annie Oakley, Wild Bill Hickok,* and *Buffalo Bill.* The exception to this rule was *The Lone Ranger,* whose popularity also extended to adults. Therefore, this show received a prime time spot at seven on Saturday evening.

After school TV time with our friends did not help us with the evening schedule, which had cutting-edge shows. Unfortunately, our creativity failed us so we merely began entering the Sigmon house without an invitation, assuming a place on the floor and watching whatever show was airing. We knew to be quiet, except for laughter, and never asked that the channel be changed. We would sigh and express disappointment when reception failed, horizontal lines scrolled rapidly, and grainy images would replace the picture. Mr. Sigmon would hobble over to the TV and with engineered precision adjust the knobs until the scrolling stopped. Then he would tiptoe back to his chair so as not to disturb the delicate balance he had achieved. In those days, viewing TV without interference was somewhat of an art.

Later in life, Sandra and I discussed this adventure, but neither could remember the first time we held this impromptu visit. Most likely our courage came in numbers, as generally seven or eight kids participated in this venturesome act. We all played outside together after dinner, and one night, powered by an overwhelming urge, we entered via the side door and situated ourselves on the floor. From that point on, it was routine. Upon leaving, we muttered "thank you" and quietly exited by the side door.

I Love Lucy aired at nine Monday nights on CBS, creating an issue for us. Preceding Lucy on CBS was the number one show, *Arthur Godfrey's Talent Scouts*. Sandra and I loved talent shows. Our desire to go to Hollywood was still strong, and we knew that a spot on a talent show would be instrumental in fulfilling that dream. We put on countless talent shows at school for anyone who would watch. Some of the scripts we wrote ourselves, but other times we would duplicate commercials.

However, channel selection depended on the Sigmons' discretion, and unfortunately for us, their taste was more refined than ours. *The Voice of Firestone*, mainly operatic singing, was on NBC opposite Arthur Godfrey and it appeared to be their favorite although, at times, they would tire of *Firestone* and turn the dial to Godfrey. Peering through the window from the shadows, we would observe Mr. Sigmon switching channels, which was our cue to walk nonchalantly through the door.

There were many shows above our intellect during the early fifties such as *Lux Video Theatre*, *Texaco Star Theatre*, and *Fireside Theatre*. The stories were difficult to follow and sometimes made no sense at all. But we loved the game shows—*Strike It Rich* and *Stop the Music*, for example—but then along came those great detective shows which have yet to be equaled, much less surpassed.

Dragnet with Detective Joe Friday was spellbinding. To this day, I'm not sure if the guy could act. He spoke in the same monotone voice, but the crooks plainly understood. His sidekick, Bill, portrayed by Harry Morgan, had a little more personality, and Harry went on to become a great comedy actor with his own show.

But our forever favorite will be *Boston Blackie*. Saturday nights at seven thirty (now considered non-primetime for TV), this handsome mustached man with dark eyes (we assumed they were dark; it was black-and-white TV) would set about solving crimes. Along with his girl pal, Mary, with help from Whitney the dog, they virtually cleaned up Los Angeles, and he wasn't even a policeman! He just arrived at the scene first or happened to be in the neighborhood and figured it all out. An early *Monk*.

Looking back, what I admired most about those shows was their ability to remain faithful to the storyline. Boston and Mary never kissed, although we kept hoping they would. Nor was there an explanation of their relationship—apparently just friends. Outside influences or extenuating relationships were not introduced on the show. It was just here is the crime, and let's get this thing solved in the next thirty minutes. In fact, I do not remember a single "continued next week" episode. These guys were brilliant!

Detective Friday and Bill operated in the same fashion—find a crime and solve it. Now, we could go to bed and not concern ourselves for a week with "whodunit." No time for extraneous or personal stuff. In fact, unless we missed it, there was never a mention of whether or not they were married. Now that is excellent script writing!

This era must have been a grand time for TV producers. New audiences were forming daily, and there was much to introduce to the world. Competition with game shows, variety, and dramas became more intense. The race for viewers spurred elaborate musicals and variety specials and introduced us to events we had only dreamed about—one being the circus. At last we were exposed to large traveling circus shows, which before were enjoyed only in larger cities. These new shows had a significant impact on our immediate life.

Until now, our circus exposure was limited to a small, one-ring circus which set up under a well-worn tent in North Newton annually. The poor animals were kept in trailers, and the smell permeated the area for blocks, lingering long after the tents were taken down. Attendees were warned to be diligent and watch for these piles when making their way to the ticket booth before entering the tent.

Still, we were impressed. Ladies dressed in faded satin bodysuits covered with torn netting caught our fancy as they raced to mount the fast-moving horses circling the ring. Trapeze artists boasted tight-fitting leotards with a few snags and opened shirts exposing hairy chests. We observed the same ladies who mounted the racing horses also rode the elephants, allowing themselves to be raised on the elephant's trunk while striking glamorous poses. Clowns ran unabashed through the seats cajoling the kids by threatening to throw pails of water which turned out to be confetti. *Yes*, we thought, *we may want to consider an exciting life in the circus.*

First, we had to decide which act we preferred so we could begin training, then hold some shows for the kids on the block. Maybe by next year when the circus rolled into town, we would be ready. After considerable thought, Sandra decided on hanging by the neck in a noose and spinning around at breakneck speed. I, on the other hand, would master the high wire. Since I am afraid of heights, this was not the best decision I have made during my lifetime.

Practice began in earnest on the pear tree in my front yard. It was not a large tree but rather skinny and not very tall, which is why we selected it. It had a bottom limb that would allow Sandra to be elevated about a foot off the ground so she could still land with ease. There were two larger limbs farther up about five feet apart for my high wire act.

The ropes proved to be more of a problem. We first tried an

old clothesline, but it was too skinny for a tight-wire and cut into Sandra's neck. Twine confiscated from Sandra's toolshed proved too weak. We hated to waste our good jump rope, since it was the only one we possessed of any length suitable for jumping doubles, but we had no choice. So we took this long, thick rope, cut it in half, and went to work.

We knew nothing about making a noose, but since our intent was not hanging oneself, we just tied a knot, making sure Sandra's head would fit, and doubled it for safety's sake. Then we took my part of the rope and climbed the tree with me on one limb and Sandra on the other. Scared to death of the height, I managed to lock my legs around the trunk and tie my end of the rope to the limb—a double knot of course. Sandra did the same, but her end barely reached, so she had to settle for one knot.

We did consider practicing but mainly concentrated on perfecting our poses before our acts and curtsies afterward. We could not figure out a method for practice without actually performing the act, so we charged ahead. Sandra went first.

I lifted her so she could slip the double-knotted noose around her neck. To ensure she would be able to rotate properly, we decided beforehand that I would give her a colossal spin before turning her loose so she could gain some speed. We got really lucky. There was just one loud scream before the limb broke. This misfortune may have saved her from a broken neck, but now there was a different problem.

Sandra had a head full of naturally curly hair, which tended to expand when exposed to wind, humidity, and other acts of nature. During the split second when I sent her on an accelerated spiral and the limb broke, her hair became entangled in the rope knot.

For a good ten minutes I tried to disentangle her hair with minimal success. Sandra was still screaming in obvious pain, so I told her I was leaving and would be back shortly with a pair of scissors. All she said was "Hurry!" I guess lying on the ground with a noose around your neck and your hair intertwined in the knot tying your body to a broken limb presents a much greater problem than having a portion of your hair cut out. All vanity was set aside.

There was not an easy way to trim her hair from this entanglement, so I merely cut it at the lowest points, lifted out the knot—hair still attached—and freed her from this difficult situation. And then she insisted I perform my act!

Grudgingly, I climbed the tree, hoping an earth-shattering event would intervene. I held tightly to the trunk while testing the rope with my summer sandals. It seemed to give a little, not very taut, but Sandra confirmed that the knots were holding. Somehow I placed both feet on the rope, still keeping one hand on the trunk, but it was futile. Without warning, both knots came undone and sent me tumbling to the ground where I landed on my back.

I do not know why we never panicked in those days—probably our sense of pride. Both of us could have been seriously injured, but we just jumped up, brushed ourselves off, silently decided the circus was not for us, and set about finding a way to put the jump rope back together.

Thanks for the memory, Sandra.

Postscript: That old pear tree was the recipient of genuinely rough treatment. It became our lookout when playing cowboys and Indians, a hiding spot for peering at the neighbors, and a short-lived home for a tire swing. I never remember it producing a single pear worth eating, and eventually it just died.

Before long, both homes were blessed with TVs, and like the rest of the country, we watched with delight. Saturday night wrestling became a popular event in our neighborhood, with neighbors selecting favorites, making bets, and threatening bodily harm on the referees. We were all brought back to reality when a neighbor became so upset one night, he ran outside and shot the antenna from his chimney.

The Sigmons, assuming that is the correct name, spent their lives in the little white house with green shutters. As I look back on the kindness of others, I regret that I did not express more gratitude and offer friendship later on in life. Distance plays a big part, I suppose, but that is an excuse and not a reason. It's been said it takes a village to raise a child, but sometimes just a block will do.

Selling Seeds

We did not enjoy winters—they were demanding—but without fail, winter welcomed spring, and we anxiously awaited and cheered for any sign that warmer, carefree days were ahead. As the days grew longer and the sun peeked over the mountains and bestowed its warmth on our faces, impatience always set in, and we tended to toss our shoes a little early to test the new grass between our toes.

Mothers and grandmothers were not immune to pushing the time frame either. On the first warm, sunny day, the heavy velvet curtains were taken from the windows and replaced with freshly washed, starched and ironed white-ruffled Priscilla curtains. Spring cleaning went into full swing with brooms and mops wielded with a vengeance. Dust flew, and cobwebs were banished from walls and ceilings, floors scrubbed, and quilts removed from the beds and beaten to an inch of their threadbare lives on the clothesline.

The coal stove, which usually resided in the middle of the central living area, was relieved of built-up ashes and scrubbed to remove all signs of soot. Then it was carefully removed and placed in an out-of-sight storage place during the spring and summer months. The flue hole in the wall was fitted with a decorative tin flue holder—usually yellow with blue flowers. It was a cleansing, as if no one wanted to be reminded of the cold, hard winters where everyone huddled in the same space for warmth and then ran to a bed full of covers—only to jump up the next morning to a cold room. Pity the early riser whose job it was to build the first fire of the day.

Sandra and I loved walking home from school on these days. It was a joy to enter our homes, now spotlessly clean with all remnants of winter removed. Along about this time, the first sign of daylilies, appropriately called Easter lilies, would poke through the tall grass and weeds. We picked them as fast as they grew and most days arrived home with a full bouquet for our playhouse.

So once it seemed that the extremes of winter had passed, it was time to prepare for the coming months. There was another yearly event which surely sealed the beginning of springtime. Each year, the elementary school participated in an annual fund-raising event: selling seed packets.

I have thought about this happening many times during my various adult careers, hoping to conjure up an equally brilliant marketing scheme. Here we had a company that packaged seeds and sold many millions of packs yearly, and their entire sales force consisted of children under the age of twelve.

The seed packs would arrive at school, and each teacher would receive enough packets to distribute ten per student. Once those packs were sold, the student turned in the money and received ten more packets. A packet of seeds cost ten cents, but I do believe that had been raised from five cents a few years earlier.

So how do you motivate children, who are much more interested in playing tag, dolls, or dodgeball or wading in the creek, to go door to door selling seeds? Simple: you offer them an incentive. This particular year the prize for the student selling the most seed packs was a Daisy air rifle for the boy (that's correct, every male kid needs an air rifle distributed by the school so he can shoot his eye out!) and a Toni doll for the girl. Both were displayed in the school cafeteria.

Toni was the brand name of the most popular home permanent which every young girl was subject to receive at least twice a year. No matter how hard the giver tried, they could never perfect this home permanent wave process, resulting in ghastly results for the receiver. However, inspired by the pictures and ads for Toni perms which were so exquisitely photographed, indicating this was an easy way to receive beautiful hair lasting for at least three months, people continued to try.

Sandra had naturally curly hair. She fought with it constantly and certainly did not need a permanent home wave. Unfortunately, one of her older sisters heard that a permanent wave had the opposite effect on naturally curly hair, resulting in a smooth, soft wave. Sandra was excited at this prospect and allowed her sister to install the permanent with the small rollers and apply the stinking solution necessary to set the curls.

If Sandra had a temper, she showed it very few times during her life, but this was an exception. She exploded! We tried everything to tame this unruly mess including Vaseline, hair tonic, and Brylcreem, but with less than desired results. Until the permanent finally worked its way out of her hair, Sandra spent most of her waking hours over the next several months with a kerchief tied around her head.

The sample Toni doll was beautiful. She came with her personal stand, had long wavy blond hair, and wore a lovely blue checked dress with matching shoes and pocketbook. She already had her fabulous perm which turned out magnificently and came with a comb and brush for styling.

We had to have this doll and quickly planned our strategy. We would work together, pool our efforts, and let one of us win the doll—but take turns keeping her, a week at a time. To do this, we would not waste our efforts on the people in our immediate neighborhood since most likely they would not have ten cents to spare. Instead, we would focus only on the larger homes in South Newton which were more apt to purchase multiple packs.

We began our quest early one Saturday morning.

Since we lived in North Newton, we had to journey to South Newton to find our prospects. So we placed our ten bags of seeds in a brown paper bag and took off on our bikes for South Newton. Once we passed the imaginary North–South boundary, the homes were more prominent, cars in every driveway and antennae on every chimney.

We scurried quickly to the first home, knocked, and waited for the door to open to give our well-rehearsed spiel: "Good morning, we are selling seed packets to raise money for our school. They are ten cents per pack, and we have flowers and vegetables. How many packs would you like?" No, we didn't come up with this speech on our own; this was all part of the training package we received, and we memorized each line. It was our first introduction to a proven sales method: always ask for the business.

The door opened, and there stood a yawning teenager with tousled hair, bare chest, wearing only boxer shorts. Before we had a chance to give our sales speech, he demanded, "What do you mean knocking on our door this early on a Saturday morning?" and slammed the door.

We looked at each other somewhat deflated. It had never occurred to us it was early on a Saturday morning. We had no reason to sleep late. In fact, just the opposite. We had goals to reach and things to accomplish.

We wandered across the street and sat on a bench in front of a church, nursing our wounds. After some time had passed, we regained our confidence and continued to the next house. This time a lady in her housecoat, curlers in her hair and coffee in her hand answered the door. Apparently, she had not been up long, but at least we had not awakened her. We gave our spiel, and she very kindly explained to us that she could not grow a weed. The green thumb had skipped her generation entirely, so she had no use for the seeds.

The next few houses brought similar responses. Then we found ourselves in front of Judge Rudisill's house—a large, two-story, white brick home by which all other dwellings were measured. Near downtown, it stood majestically with tall columns on the porch and a long pendant light in the center. The yard was always perfectly manicured, and giant ferns filled the urns on either side of the door. We walked up the entryway with hearts pounding.

We knocked timidly on the large door which was soon opened by a regal-looking lady. Her black hair was pulled back in a bun with not a hair out of place and makeup expertly applied. She was fully dressed this early Saturday morning in a spring suit with high heels. We were more than intimidated; we were speechless. Before we could regain our composure or run, as we considered doing, she looked at us gently and smiled. "Oh, so you are selling seeds for your school?"

"Yes, ma'am," I replied.

Sandra added, "And we have flowers and vegetables." We were completely thrown off guard and forgot our spiel entirely.

"Are they still ten cents a pack?" she asked. And when we both nodded yes, she said, "Then I'll take a pack of each."

We did not walk from that house, we skipped. We had met Mrs. Rudisill, and she was lovely! That's how we wanted to be—sophisticated and ready to greet the world at any time. Did she sleep fully dressed and made up?

We now had a new approach to selling, so with all trepidation aside, we ran eagerly to the next house. Boldly we knocked on the door with a little more confidence, chests out and ready to give our sales speech as soon as the door opened. But we didn't, because before us stood the meanest man we had ever encountered who without provocation launched into a tirade about the dozens of kids who had already come by selling seeds and the stupidity of the school system for allowing this! "We pay taxes," he inserted, "so why do they have to raise money? They should spend it on education and not all of these extracurricular activities like bands and football. Our generation is on an inevitable path to total ruin!" With that he slammed the door.

Dear Lord! What just happened? Shoulders slumped, discouraged and hurt by the brutality of this man, we slowly walked away. We never said anything to one another about heading back to North Newton. We just walked in unison toward home. It seemed safer to be in familiar territory, and after some thought, we realized we had not seen a single garden planted in a side or backyard in South Newton, but in our part of town, almost everyone sowed a small garden, while others planted an entire field.

As we headed home, we selectively stopped at homes we knew had gardens or at least friendly people inside. We heard various reasons for not buying, such as "I've already ordered from the Burpee catalog" or "I haven't decided if I am going to plant a garden this year" or a favorite, "Come back next week when I get paid."

We managed to sell a few more packs of seeds, although not nearly enough to compete for the prizes, but the lessons were priceless. Always ask for the business, it will take a multitude of nos to get a yes, and there are good people in every part of town.

I don't know who won the Daisy air rifle as we had little interest in that prize. A girl from South Newton won the Toni doll, probably because her family bought tons of seeds (of course, this was mere speculation on our part). We also felt misled. We assumed the contest was for our elementary school only, not the whole school system!

Thanks for the memory, Sandra.

Postscript: Judge Rudisill's house still stands majestically, and whenever I return to Newton, I always ride by, slow down, and admire its presence. Judge Rudisill's son, with his wife, made this their home after his parents' deaths. Now they too are deceased, and the house is undergoing renovation. Hopefully, it will remain home to a family for many years to come.

I can still see Mrs. Rudisill standing in the doorway, the epitome of a truly graceful Southern lady. It meant a lot to those two little girls that morning that she smiled so kindly and purchased those two packs of seeds. I hope the seeds produced beautiful flowers and hearty vegetables, but I doubt if that was her purpose.

Tent Revivals and Homecomings

I am not sure what we aspired to be during our preteen years, other than famous, but for sure our religious environment played a large part in our attempt to decide on a career path. Our love for gospel music was intense, especially for Southern gospel quartets. We loved the four-part harmony with crescendo pitches, celebrated worship songs and could not resist an altar call during "Just as I Am."

We practiced blending our voices constantly but struggled with who would tackle soprano and who would be granted the alto part. Our voice ranges landed us both in the alto section, but someone had to sing soprano, so the task of reaching those high notes was left to me. Sandra was much more musically inclined than I, so it was only fair that most concessions would go to her when it came to music.

We intended to make our debut by singing at different churches, thereby gaining experience which would lead to performances at funerals and revivals. Our first opportunity to launch our career presented itself when a traveling tent revival pitched camp in our neighborhood.

Tent revivals were not uncommon during our developmental years. Traveling tent meetings could be spotted throughout the South in small towns and rural areas. A large truck would roll into town, pitch a tent, and post signs on telephone poles announcing location and times. Volunteers distributed flyers to churches with similar beliefs, and posters were displayed in business windows. We were excited when we spotted a truck pulling into the vacant lot on the next block behind the Lackey house, about a thirty-second walk for us. It had to be an omen!

Practice began in earnest. Tent revivals traveled with a skeleton crew requiring everyone to perform double or triple duty. Most did not travel with gospel singers and depended on local talent. Nightly the preacher or staff member would ask for volunteers to take the stage and sing a special.

At this time in our life, our experience was limited to the Knapp Shoe tent we played in as youngsters or practicing in front of the mirror. We had yet to take the stage but were full of confidence—plus, it appeared relatively easy.

We decided on a beautiful song, quite a favorite among gospel singers at the time, "When God Dipped His Pen of Love in My Heart." This song had four verses and a chorus, all of which we intended to complete. We would carry our hymnal to the stage but only as a prop. For maximum exposure, we would sing all four verses plus the chorus after each verse all the while facing the audience—just like the Statesmen Quartet!

We practiced for hours daily the week before. Then, on Monday, the first night of the revival, we walked into the tent and took a seat on the first row for easy access to the stage. The preacher led the congregation in several old hymns, pausing to pray after each one. Then he politely asked if anyone would like to take the stage and perform a special song. We both froze, and before we could recover, he launched into a fire and brimstone sermon striking the fear of eternal damnation on the congregation. We ignored the altar call and quietly slipped out the side of the tent.

However, we returned the next night and the next, and so on, determined to overcome our stage fright. Finally, the last night of the revival arrived. We had practiced all week, observed the congregation, and decided there was no threat. So we boldly walked up to the preacher before services and asked if we could sing a special song. He was thrilled. He also noted our devout attendance during the revival and felt sure the congregation would enjoy our duet.

When the service started, butterflies began immediately. We were trying desperately to produce a reason to forgive our commitment. Other than running, a strong consideration, we could not come up with an alternative. Then he announced that two young girls on the front row who had attended service each night would like to perform a song for this spirited congregation and motioned for us to take the stage.

We stood up slowly, our legs like rubber, palms sweating, neither of us sure anything would come out once we opened our mouths. We paused by the piano, gave the pianist the name of our song, and she politely explained the last sentence in the chorus would serve as our lead-in. We turned to the audience briefly but quickly focused our eyes on the songbook. With our hearts racing as she finished the intro, we began singing in what was barely a whisper.

Our intent was to sing all four verses, but after one verse and one chorus, without conferring with each other, we turned and walked off the stage with the pianist still playing. The preacher thanked us, as did some people in the row behind us, which helped keep our embarrassment to a minimum. Now if only we could get through another one of his sermons!

But as days passed and our braggadocio grew, we concluded it was a decent performance, if in need of some polishing. We decided to continue with our plan to seek other avenues for our talent. There were many churches in our vicinity—Baptist, Methodist, Church of God, and Pentecostal Holiness plus several independents. By vicinity, I mean within walking distance, as this was our main mode of transportation.

Parallel to our neighborhood on the other side of Main Street were several churches including the Holiness church where my grandfather once served as a pastor. Nearby was a Church of God which we had visited several times with friends. This particular church was quite strict in their beliefs, but they held the most glorious homecomings and all-day singings.

Homecomings happened once a year. They were times when members, former members, and pastors came together for all-day services, singing, and eating. The women of the church rose early to prepare their most requested dishes for the homecoming spread. After morning service, long tables were assembled on the church grounds to display the food. All day singing and eating were topped off by an evening service.

We attended these homecomings each time we heard one was scheduled at this Church of God. On this particular homecoming day, we had enjoyed all the activities when someone from the congregation invited us to stay for evening services. We knew this person's daughter and son, and they begged us to remain by indicating there was a unique service that night. Curious, and since we had partaken of their food, we felt obliged to attend.

The church that evening was set up differently. The pulpit had been moved to the side clearing the raised stage. On the stage were folding chairs lined on both sides. Expecting a play or dramatic event, we seated ourselves in the second row from the front.

It wasn't long after service began that it dawned on us what was happening. We had committed ourselves to participate in a foot washing!

We had heard about foot washings but had never observed or participated in one. Foot washings held in religions such as Catholic and Episcopalian, seem to take on a more somber and formal tone. As we were about to find out, this would not be the case at our foot washing.

Now Sandra and I had worries. First, we had on sandals and had been running and walking in the dirt all day, so our feet were filthy. But Sandra was terrified because she had a much deeper concern. Sandra only had nine toes! That's right—just *nine!*

It was a well-kept secret between the two of us. Besides Sandra's family, she did not care for anyone else to learn of this defect. Kids tended to tease, and adults asked too many questions, so it was just best to avoid the issue. It was hard to keep it a secret during the summer due to going barefoot, wearing sandals and such, but Sandra had perfected methods for hiding this imperfection.

There was nothing weird about it; she wasn't born that way. It was just that one day when she was three or four, Sandra decided to help her dad chop wood, unsupervised. Unfortunately, she missed the chopping stump, and the ax fell on her foot, severing her little toe. She was rushed to the hospital, and bandaged. Then, poor thing, upon returning home she fell through the glass door, inflicting a cut on her face, and returned to the hospital.

So you can see that with her inhibitions about having nine toes, she could not bear to expose this difference in a church, on a stage with a large audience watching. This time our tendency to sit up front close to the action betrayed us. All of a sudden, before we could conjure up an escape plan, a gentleman stood at the end of our pew and instructed us to rise and go to the stage. Unbeknownst to us, participants in the foot washing had been asked to sit on the first two rows!

There were two rows of five straight chairs with a wash pan and pitcher at the bottom of each chair. We were led to the right, seated side by side, and instructed to remove our shoes. With shoes removed, our feet presented a perfect outline where our white sandals once resided. A sister placed our feet in the dishpan, poured cool water over them, and began washing and muttering a Bible verse while the minister read scripture and the organist played.

The same thing was happening to Sandra, but suddenly her sister turned to mine and exclaimed in a not-so-soft tone, "She only has nine toes!" This announcement would not have been too bad as the people in the congregation probably could not hear except all the other brothers and sisters ceased their ceremonies to gather around Sandra's wash pan. There they stared in astonishment, thereby engaging the congregation's attention.

I could sense Sandra's embarrassment, but she was also seething. Finally, someone asked, "What happened to your toe?"

She answered bluntly in a not-so-soft voice, "I chopped it off with an ax!" They all winced as cold chills ran up their spines, but it silenced them.

The sisters handed the wash pans to those assisting, who ran to the side door and threw the dirty water into the yard. Sandra and I grabbed our shoes, explained we needed to get home by dark, and hurried out the back door. It was our first and last foot washing but not the end of our singing.

Thanks for the memory, Sandra.

Postscript: We never gave up on our amateur singing. We joined the choir, formed a quartet, and often sang in church. We were members of the glee club in high school and took part in many competitions. It was a significant part of our lives.

Sandra got over her issue with nine toes and used the accidental phenomenon to her advantage by pulling many jokes on people. In fact, during her bout with cancer, a hospital attendant rounded a curve too fast with her hospital bed and ran into the wall. She proclaimed her foot was in extreme pain and thought he had injured her toe. When he pulled back the sheet and saw the foot was missing a toe, he almost fainted.

Rooftop Views

An earlier memory introduced the tin roof over the garage harboring our playhouse. The roof had a pitch which tapered and joined a flat roof extension. It was on the extension that a branch from the apple tree overhung, allowing access to our private observatory. It enabled us to scale the tree and crawl along the branch onto the roof. My fear of heights brought many anxious moments, primarily when it was time to retreat down the tree limb, but with Sandra's encouragement, we spent time almost daily during warm months on top of the roof.

Tin roofs are extraordinarily hot when the sun shines directly on the surface. However, in the shade or without direct sun, they quickly take on the same temperature as the surrounding air. The limb provided enough shade for us to sit comfortably once in place, and we had the good sense to throw a quilt across the hot areas. Without direct sun exposure, the roof presented us with a comfortable, panoramic view of the neighbors and their activities. We would sit for hours and observe a plethora of neighborhood antics.

A family had moved into the corner house opposite us. There were several children—both older and younger than us— and although we attended the same elementary school, they never took part in neighborhood exploits. In fact, the family was somewhat reclusive. I barely remember the father, but the mother stayed home and spent most of her time peering out the front window with gospel music blaring from the radio.

Sandra and I watched this lady while on the roof and were

somewhat perplexed by her activities. She began her day staring from the front window, but if she noticed something or someone on the side road, she would move to the side window. She made it her business to condemn people walking by for wearing too much makeup or a dress bodice cut too low by calling them Jezebel and warning them of a future burning in hell. In spite of her self-righteousness, we never saw the family attend church.

We watched these events with interest while trying to understand her purpose. The neighborhood had become quite enthralled with her actions and sometimes hostile, referring to her as a nosy old biddy, a gossipy nag, and a hypocrite.

Finally, Sandra and I figured that if we could identify an underlying reason for her actions, perhaps we could resolve the unrest in the neighborhood. However, to complete our detective work, we needed access to the interior of the house, which required us to make friends with one of the children.

The youngest of the children was four or five years old and seemed to be the easiest prey. The older brother was mean and called us names; quite frankly, we were afraid of him. The older sister was timid and seldom came outside. The youngest, however, played on the back stoop, which had an entry into an empty coal bin. (When homes had coal stoves, the houses were built with a room outside for storing and sheltering coal from the elements.) This sister regularly went in and out of the empty coal bin.

So one afternoon, our courage in tow, we ambled across the street and up the back drive to the stoop. We asked the sister, "What are you doing?"

"Playing," she replied. We dove right in, asking questions and permission to play also. The coal bin was dark and still smelled of soot. There were a few old pieces of furniture, some trash, and a couple of shelves holding cardboard boxes marked "JELL-O BUTTERSCOTCH PUDDING MIX."

The sister stood in the coal bin holding an open box of the butterscotch pudding. Suddenly, the pieces began falling into place. The neighbors often spoke of this little sister and the constant crust formed around her mouth. They connected the coating to her fragility and ongoing stomach pains. In fact, the neighbor next door had seized an opportunity to wash the girl's mouth only to observe it was crusty again a few hours later. It was feared she had some type of dread disease, perhaps leprosy! At least we had solved this mystery: the poor girl spent most of her time eating old powdered butterscotch pudding mix most likely filled with bugs.

Still feeling the need to enter the house to complete our investigation on her mother, we asked the sister if we could use the bathroom. Without objection, she led us through the kitchen door to the back hall and pointed to a door. The kitchen was bare, with only a table and a couple chairs. We saw a stove but no refrigerator. There were two beds in the bedroom we passed, and we caught a glimpse of a couch in the living room. We could hear the mother moving around, but when we heard footsteps headed toward us and someone screaming, "Who's there?" we decided we did not need to use the bathroom after all.

We scurried quickly out the back door, jumped off the porch, and headed down the drive with the mother waving a Bible and yelling after us to stay away and never come back, lest we face eternal ruin.

Returning to safety, we now took time to analyze our discoveries. Indeed, the sister should not be eating boxes and boxes of outdated dry pudding. The mother, on the other hand, didn't have anything to do, and we were pretty sure demons possessed her. Our mothers cleaned, cooked, washed, ironed, and so on, but there was very little to do in this house. We determined she was just bored, lazy, unstable, and a little "off her rocker." So we analyzed all that happened and presented our report to my mother and a couple of her friends gathered on the front porch.

The news spread like wildfire with every person within a mile circumference alerted before dinnertime of the atrocities in this house. With each retelling, the story grew and worsened until it reached the point that someone called the welfare department (now known as Social Services), and somehow, the police got involved. Commotion ensued and lasted for days in that corner house. The children were crying and calling us names, and the mother was cursing all the neighbors. Could Sandra and I have misinterpreted the situation? The grown-ups reassured us that we'd done the right thing by reporting our findings to adults, so we just shelved any misgivings and assumed the role of heroes.

It all ended one day when the family began packing their belongings and loaded the boxes on their father's truck. They made several trips somewhere, with the children doing most of the work. The mother, on the other hand, walked up and down the street, pausing in front of any neighbor's home where she felt there was involvement, and began singing and, paraphrasing to fit the moment, an old gospel tune, "Will There Be Any Stars in Your Crown?"

Postscript: We never knew what happened to the family on the corner. The children did not return to our school, so we theorized they had moved out of the city limits. Sandra and I were always a little guilty that we had caused trouble for the family. As we matured, it was obvious this was a destitute family struggling to survive on the barest essentials in an unstable home. As youngsters, I am not sure what we could have done considering the times, but we often wished we had interpreted our visit differently.

I mentioned in an earlier memory an incident we observed on top of the same tin roof but needed to muster my courage to write about it. By today's standards, it isn't too bad, but as for Sandra and me, we were embarrassed, aghast, curious, and—well, I will admit it brought us plenty of laughter through the years.

Just where the slanted tin roof met the extension was a perfect resting place for us, resembling an elongated lounge chair. We would sit in this spot under the branch, which offered seclusion, and watch all events and unusual behavior in the neighborhood. We saw many things that were not intended for human eyes, which may explain why we insisted on closing blinds and curtains in our homes as adults.

Our section of the roof faced a small house where a couple lived with their grown daughter. She was already in high school or perhaps had graduated, making her much older than us. She never socialized with her peers in the neighborhood but did seem to have an active social life and quite a few boyfriends.

Both parents worked, but the daughter remained home during the day cleaning and doing laundry and other chores. Her bedroom window faced our rooftop observatory, giving us a clear view inside. It was summertime, and without air-conditioning, windows were always raised and curtains pulled back to allow air to circulate.

On this particular day, we had climbed atop the roof early, enjoying the shade while sipping lemonade and relishing an apple picked from the tree. We noticed a car parked in the driveway of the house in front of us, and soon we saw movement in the girl's bedroom. The shade was not drawn, and the curtains were spread wide, so our view, although narrow, was not obstructed.

We became focused on our slender window view and eventually were able to see the girl and a boy wandering in and out of our sight. With the curtains blowing in the wind, our view was obstructed at times, so we slid down to the edge of our tin roof for a closer look. Curiously enough, layers of their clothing seemed to be slowly disappearing as they meandered in and out of our vantage point.

Suddenly, common sense rained down on us at the same time as we realized the significance of what was happening. Even worse, as good Christian girls, we were overcome with shame for even stumbling across this happening, although it was not explicit, so we swiftly scrambled from the hot tin roof to reach the limb, crossed to the trunk of the tree, and shimmied to the ground. Then we ran to the front porch and out of sight.

Fortunately, we had little contact with this grown girl, so we never knew if we had been caught watching their actions. We laughed about this many times—sometimes wishing we had not covered our eyes! But having been raised in religious families, at the time we felt watching was as sinful as doing.

Thanks for the memory, Sandra.

Strawberry Fields Forever

We were now in the sixth grade at Thornton Elementary. Sandra and I were very much at home in this school, built three years earlier for the children in North Newton, thereby separating us from the South Newton kids who soon would have their own elementary school as well. However, we would all merge again at Newton Elementary for the seventh and eighth grades and continue for four years at Newton-Conover High School. Middle school and junior high were still in the future.

Thornton Elementary was built to newer standards for that era. All on one level, it had covered walkways to the detached cafeteria and gyms, with all classrooms feeding into a common interior long hallway. Each classroom had an outside entrance/exit, propelling us ahead of our time for safety standards and easy access to the playgrounds. The building had a midcentury modern design, and bright colored panels and rollout windows added to its futuristic facade. We were quite proud of our new school.

Most children were from either our neighborhood or nearby areas and attended our church or patronized the same places. It was much closer to our home, so the walk to and from school was not nearly as far. However, once we discovered a creek running behind the houses opposite the school, we quickly wasted any gained time by playing in the stream on the way home.

Free from the shackles of social inferiority, we found ourselves taking the lead in a multitude of activities. Our teacher, Mr. Gomedela, also served as principal, so the first part of the morning he spent in the office taking care of business, leaving our class unsupervised during those early hours.

Still harboring the Hollywood bug, now exacerbated due to TVs in our homes, we took on the role of writing and presenting shows in the music room for anyone who wished to attend. These theatrical presentations ran the gamut from detective dramas to humor to variety shows. To mimic TV as closely as possible, we included commercials.

Our commercials included floating a bar of Ivory soap in an attempt to solidify their claim of "So pure it floats"—for a second, anyway; then it sank to the bottom of the shallow dishpan. We sang the jingle to Pepsi-Cola, holding a bottle of the beverage and proclaiming proudly, "Say Pepsi, please" and "For those who think young." Cigarettes could not be ignored, and we provided plenty of these commercials, encouraging our fellow sixth-graders to "light up." But our favorite, which we featured almost daily, was belting out the tune sung by Dinah Shore, "See the USA in your Chevrolet." As we sang, we pointed out attractions on the pull-down map of the United States.

But our proudest achievement in the sixth grade was forming a Tony Curtis Fan Club. We were just absolutely smitten by Tony Curtis. We had no idea how to join a fan club or whether or where one existed—so we just decided to form our own.

Notebook in hand, we set about asking our friends if they would like to join our fan club. Most said yes immediately. A few asked questions which we could not answer, but we promised to address those concerns at the first meeting.

The meeting was held on top of the large culvert pipe which ran through the playground to channel water toward the creek. A large part of the pipe was uncovered, and students used it for many activities. The boys were always challenging each other to crawl from one end to the other (about half the length of a football field), but after one reckless student, who could never resist a dare, had to outcrawl a snake midway through, that activity ceased. Playgrounds were not well supervised during our school years.

So we all gathered on a designated day, with Sandra and I already in place as self-proclaimed president and vice president. Since we formed the club, we certainly would not be giving up those offices. There were probably eight to ten friends present. It was lunchtime, so we were pressed to accomplish much in a few minutes. After spending a few of those minutes drooling over our idol, we turned to business.

We decided on one rule that day: anyone who was a member of the Tony Curtis Fan Club in North Newton was obligated to see *every* movie he starred in from this day forward. It was a simple enough rule and one we looked forward to obeying.

So it was only a few weeks later that a member mentioned that *Six Bridges to Cross* starring Tony Curtis was now playing at the Newton Theater!

Newton had two theaters: the State Theater on College Street in town, and the Newton Theater on Brady Avenue, one street behind College Avenue. The Newton Theater was newer, and the seating was better. We were thrilled.

There was just one problem. We had no money. Admission, as I recall, was twelve cents for ages twelve and under. Although Sandra exceeded the age limit by a few months and I was nearing my birthday, we were still able to get the twelve-cent rate by bending our knees, making ourselves appear shorter as we approached the ticket box. Certainly twelve cents is not much today, but as someone (like our mothers) pointed out, that was a pair of socks, or a loaf of bread, or a bag of pinto beans. (Mothers have the strangest way of making a point.) It became clear that if we wanted to see this movie; we needed to earn some money. Quick!

The idea came to us as we walked home one afternoon. Crossing Main Street, we noticed that the grocery store next to the service station on the corner seemed to be having an outdoor sale. A closer look showed that the store had set up produce stands outside with different vendors selling fresh fruit and veggies. The most enticing stand was the strawberry stand, and one basket was fifteen cents. We would only have to sell two baskets and would have money left over!

We knew where the strawberries grew; we had passed the field many times on our way to Two Joe Hill on our bikes. Now we just had to turn right on the dirt road rather than left on the paved road. We would package our pickings in paper bags, as we were without baskets or any clue where to get them. Our plan was set for Saturday morning. If we did well, we might even make the movie that afternoon.

Saturday morning we set out on our bikes with two large buckets swinging from the handlebars, one from each home where they were used to mop floors. It was all we could find. A furniture plant was located in the fork where the street turned left leading to Two Joe Hill. To the right was a dirt road, which quickly turned into desolation and large fields. We took a right turn.

We could see a couple of homes at the far end of the fields, but mainly it was desolate. We disembarked from our bikes and grabbed our buckets. We had traveled this road before and always noticed the wild strawberries. Although low growing, they seemed to be plentiful. In fact, the field was huge!

We attacked the strawberry patch with vigor, but these fragile fruits were so small, it was necessary to pick them delicately to avoid crushing. After what seemed like hours of steady picking, the bottoms of our buckets were barely covered with strawberries. We had only eaten a few, but this could take forever.

We adjusted our strategy by sitting and scooting along rather than stooping. The sun was almost straight up and bearing down when Sandra came up with a better idea: we would pull the low growing vines, bringing up many at once, and then sit and pick in the shade. The closest shade was near the back edge, but we could pull the vines as we crossed the field and gather strawberries after we reached the shade. It was more efficient, and before long we each had picked about a half bucket.

Still determined to sell, get the money, and make the movie, we decided to bag what we had and only charge thirteen cents. We could do without a soft drink. So we were headed home with our bucket of strawberries swinging from our handlebars when we spotted an old red pickup truck turning down the dirt road. The truck slowed as it neared, and a bearded man, with a tooth missing and a dirty baseball cap, stuck his head out the window and asked, "What you girls got in those buckets?"

Simultaneously, we answered, "Wild strawberries."

"Wild strawberries! You know those things are poisonous. Hope you didn't eat any!"

We pedaled furiously, reaching my house in less than ten minutes. We threw the buckets on the ground and just stared at each other. We had munched on strawberries all morning and would surely die! *Should we tell someone? No, we'll only get in more trouble.* So we ditched the strawberries in the vacant field next door, put the pails back where they belonged, and sat down to ponder our fate.

How long we would live, how painful the death would be— we didn't know. Thank goodness we had been attending church regularly. But worst of all, we would miss the movie.

Thanks for the memory, Sandra.

Postscript: *Only a few hours later the itching began, and we had to confess where we had been all day to acquire all those chigger bites.*

We wished many times we could identify the bearded man. He ruined our whole day, not to mention putting an end to the North Newton Tony Curtis Fan Club. As we found out later, wild strawberries are not at all poisonous and are highly desired for their flavor. Most likely he was thinking of mushrooms.

The Newton Theater closed many years ago, but as of this date, the State Theater in the heart of downtown still exists and now has multiple screens. It is still a fun evening for residents to eat at a local restaurant and walk across the street for a movie. Neither of us ever saw Six Bridges to Cross. *Maybe it will be on TV someday.*

Worst Summer Ever

The first case of polio was diagnosed in Hickory, a town about twelve miles from Newton, in 1944. Within twenty-four hours there were six more cases in Hickory and sixty-four more in the area. The next few years brought a devastating epidemic, which peaked in 1948 and continued into the early 1950s. Our county, Catawba, was the hardest hit in the nation.

On our few blocks alone, there were four polio victims, resulting in the death of a playmate, another severely crippled, and one spending her life in an iron lung. During the peak summer, all social venues were closed, including the pools. Any gathering, especially if it involved children, was discouraged, and since initially it was thought the polio virus was transferred via rivers and streams, access to those were denied when possible and otherwise strongly discouraged.

Counties imposed quarantines for children, prohibiting travel from county to county. This quarantine was quite upsetting to my sister and me; we were scheduled to spend the summer at my grandparents' home in North Wilkesboro a couple of counties away. Too upset not to go, we hid in the back seat as we approached the county line, fully expecting to see guards holding rifles, but there were no officers, so we continued and spent a couple of weeks with our grandparents.

Upon returning home, Sandra and I became depressed that friends we knew had contracted this horrible disease. It was also sad that activities we enjoyed during usual carefree summer months were now on hiatus, so most days we found ourselves sitting on my front porch steps wallowing in self-pity. It was during one of these grumbling sessions that the idea came to us: We would take up tap dancing and put on a Broadway show for the neighborhood and passersby!

My front porch, constructed of wood planks, albeit worn and in need of painting, ran the length of the house with four posts, one on each end and others on each side of the center steps. A perfect stage! We planned to hang confiscated sheets and worn-out curtains between the posts on each side, leaving the middle as our stage. The house faced a busy road, so our audience could conceivably be huge! We challenged our playmates to spread the word and encourage everyone to assemble for the show in a couple of hours.

Prompted by the variety shows on TV, we had developed a serious interest in tap dancing, inspired also by the fact that lessons were being offered at the downtown community center—if one's parents could afford it. No one in our neighborhood could, but a classmate of ours was enrolled. On the days when the tap class was scheduled after school, she would bring tap shoes with her and allow Sandra and me to take turns practicing our improvised tap dancing along with basic steps she taught us. We were hooked.

We savored those days with access to tap shoes, so when our classmate mentioned she was getting a new pair of shoes and would be selling her old ones, we immediately began saving our money, giving her a nickel or dime as a down payment to ensure she would hold them for us. Layaways were popular during our youth, so we considered this a simple business transaction. We were hoping to have the full amount by the time school reconvened in the fall and prayed the shoes would not be too tight by then.

However, future plans were of no benefit to us on this day. We needed to fix the stage, improvise tap shoes, and begin rehearsals.

Our song selection was limited to the few 78 rpm records on hand, most of which had been given to my mother by friends. We did possess an old record player, but it was in dire need of a new needle. As a result, the outgoing sound was scratchy, and the volume was low, but we considered this a minor issue.

Unfortunately, most of the songs on the albums were slow and romantic. One particular album did include "Chattanooga Choo Choo," "Boogie Woogie Bugle Boy," and our favorite, an upbeat version of "Side By Side." We were now set: three songs and three dances to choreograph.

We draped old sheets to conceal the porch area and our rehearsal and preparation, which led us to creating our tap shoes. Fortunately, it was about this time that toe and heel taps became popular with teenage boys. Originally intended to prevent wear and tear on the toes and heels of shoes, the taps made a sound that took hold on the current youthful male generation and became a symbol of "cool."

Real taps were moon shaped and fastened to the shoe with tiny brads; the job was best done at a shoe shop. I only remember one shoe shop in Newton, and suddenly this small business was inundated with young men intent on announcing their entrance and existence to everyone within earshot.

Those who could not afford real taps were not to be outdone and were forced to rely on their creativity. Our brothers had fallen into this category and had successfully created taps from bottle caps. This made sense, as the ruffled edge of the cap was sharp and could be pounded into rubber soles and heels. It was a good option and worked quite well.

Bottle caps were easy to find. Litter laws were nonexistent, so people discarded bottle caps on the ground, on sidewalks, or on roads where they became embedded in the asphalt. Within minutes we had gathered a handful of bottle caps in various sizes.

Sandals were the only summer shoes we possessed except for our Sunday church shoes, which were not the popular Mary Janes of this time but did resemble them. For a moment we did ponder that trouble might arise from attaching bottle caps to our Sunday shoes, but as always, we managed to rationalize our decision and set about adding taps to our fake Mary Janes.

It was more difficult than we thought. It seemed the soles of boys' shoes were much thicker and could accommodate the sharp edge. Conversely, our shoes had slim leather soles, and the hammering tended to bend the bottle cap. Then we remembered that the shoe shop attached taps to the shoes with tiny brads.

Rummaging through the shed where Sandra's father kept his tools, we grabbed nails we hoped would solve our problem. The first nail penetrated the bottle cap and pierced through the top of the shoe. We had essentially nailed the shoe together. Still, we forged ahead!

Working in tandem, we soon each had a shoe with a hole out the top; we would tackle that problem later with thick shoe polish. We had successfully managed to attach bottle caps to the heels but still lacked a solution for the toe taps when we were overcome with brilliance. The top of a tin can may do the trick. It was already rounded, so we could fold it in half and then trim to fit. It might work better than bottle caps as the can top would consist of two layers and possibly tap louder.

Rummaging through the garbage can at both houses, we searched until we found the smallest tin can tops. We folded the tops in the middle and hammered them flat. Now the only chore remaining was to trim and attach them. Trimming was difficult, as our only tool was a pair of dull scissors; after some time, we realized this was futile. The tin can top only folded over the toe of the sole about a half inch, so we decided to leave it; after all, it was barely noticeable.

Now, how to attach our new toe taps to the shoes? Nailing again was out of the question, so we settled on glue. We had spotted an old can labeled GLUE in Sandra's shed. Ignoring directions, we applied the glue liberally and set a brick on each shoe to aid in adherence. It was an excellent time to pull out the record player, set up the stage, and put finishing touches on our routine.

There were only a few steps in our repertoire: shuffle, hop, and hop shuffle step. We varied these standard steps somewhat and threw in a few others we had seen performed on TV involving turns, swaying side to side, and a rather sad version of flap ball change. It would suffice, and the rest we would improvise. With rehearsal time limited, we decided only the opening needed to be performed in unison. Then, we would go solo by yielding the stage to each other where we would freestyle.

In need of costumes suitable for this performance, we exchanged our everyday shorts for a dress with a full ruffled skirt, which seemed more appropriate. Regretting that we did not have a tutu or a costume with bounce, we simply tucked the hemmed skirt of our dress under the elastic of our underwear, creating a large, flouncy pouf.

Our playmates had done a good job of marketing our production, but now our siblings and the neighborhood kids were hanging around waiting for this production. They were growing restless and making rude comments. Annoyed, we were being pushed into an early curtain time, we announced we were ready to go. Someone volunteered to start the music while I hid behind one covered side and Sandra the other. Then we each made our debut with a toe heel tap until we met in the middle and turned to face the audience.

First mishap: my bottle cap came off my heel, so we had to stop for repairs but restarted with minimal delay. Next, the music began skipping because our heavy tapping jarred the record player. Simple fix: we just moved the record player behind the screen door and restarted the performance. Again, our audience was getting fidgety, which irritated us.

The third or maybe the fourth start was better. We completed a couple of verses of "Side By Side" before our tin can tops started to unglue and began flapping. The elastic in our panties was having a hard time supporting our skirts, and we could feel our makeshift tutus sliding downward. Cars slowed down to watch this spectacle, some coming to a stop, others blowing their horns, but all engaged in laughter. Our friends were rolling in the grass laughing, especially the boys.

We endured all the bad reviews, but the last straw came when we overheard my mother, with her head stuck out the window and telephone receiver in her hand, call her friend Dessie across the street and say, "Dessie, come over quick! You have got to see this—it's the funniest thing ever!" We expected it from the obnoxious boys in the neighborhood, but *my mother*?

Deflated, we stomped off the stage, told everyone to leave, and announced the show was over. Sure, maybe it was a crude mess, but at least we offered an activity for this otherwise dull summer day. Improvisation surely made up for the lack of talent and props. And besides, there was nothing else to do!

Then a jarring yet familiar reminder from my mother: "You girls be sure and clean up your mess!"

Thanks for the memory, Sandra.

Postscript: Those of us growing up during this period still recount the desperation felt during the polio epidemic. We received our first immunization, gamma globulin, which held out hope as a cure but was short-lived. Thankfully, Dr. Jonas Salk discovered the Salk vaccine which became mandatory for public school children and virtually wiped out polio internationally. There were many heroes born of this epidemic, and it is well worth learning more. Here is an excellent link on the subject: http://hickoryart.org/new-blog/2015/4/7/ the-miracle-of-hickory-the-1944-polio-hospital

Sandra and I kept our tap dancing aspirations open for quite a while. However, we never received the tap shoes from our classmate. By the time we saved enough money, they were too small, and she had already passed them along to someone else.

Halloween and the Wall

We skipped merrily through our elementary school years, enjoying the brisk walks necessary to arrive at school before the tardy bell rang but lingering in the afternoons by the creek, which we justified by deeming it a shortcut. Many times we lost track of time and found ourselves in trouble, but the light punishment never fit the crime, and we continued to spend many afternoons at the creek.

During our school tenure, elementary included first through eighth grade followed by four years of high school. We had several neighborhood schools that took us through the sixth grade, but we all converged on the largest elementary school in town for seventh and eighth grades. Consequently, we had solid friendships during early elementary years and new ones when we entered seventh grade through graduation.

It was around the sixth or seventh grade when we welcomed another friend, Kay. Kay lived within a block or two of both Sandra and me, and we could all meet on the corner for our walk to school, church, or downtown. Kay was a very pretty girl with an enviable wardrobe. Her aunt owned an upscale dress shop in town, and Kay worked some on weekends and took advantage of the employee and relative discounts. She was always the best-dressed girl in school, with perfect skin and hair. In spite of her impeccable looks and taste, Kay was also fun-loving in an innocent way and consequently felt right at home on our excursions.

By now, our interests were more developed. We no longer

were chasing movie stars or nursing circus aspirations. Having been exposed to a grander view of our town and attending school with the more affluent South Newton population, we now sought more mature antics.

It was during lunch and recess breaks at school that we overheard the boys discussing pranks they had played on Halloween nights. Our Halloween tricks to date were limited to moving a garbage can to the front porch, removing clothes from the clothesline, etc. (One time we did relieve ourselves in the neighbor's bushes out of necessity.) The boys raised our imagination to a new level, and so this upcoming Halloween we vowed to perform a real, grown-up prank.

The North Newton Baptist Church was on a corner in our neighborhood. Kay was already a member, and for some reason, Sandra and I decided we would be better served if we joined this church. The distance was only a short walk, and many of our friends were members. So on our own, we joined the church and were both baptized in the baptismal behind the choir section.

The church was a major part of our life. Brick and stone, it sat on the corner and became a staple in our lives. Throughout our high school years, we were very faithful and heavily involved in Sunday school, youth groups, and the choir. Never losing our love for gospel music, we formed a girls' quartet and sometimes united with our brothers' male quartet.

The church had a brick retaining wall along the sidewalk with steps leading to the grounds. On either side of the steps were large juniper bushes which could snag your hose.

On this particular Halloween, the city was performing roadwork directly in front of those steps. The crew had removed the pavement and dug a hole about four feet by six on the left side, exposing the manhole cover. Smudge pots and crossbars surrounded the hole, with signs directing drivers to use the right lane so as not to drive into the hole and damage their front end.

As we were wandering around on this Halloween night searching for mischief that would match the level of our male peers, we came upon the roadwork in front of the church. I don't know who came up with the idea first, but in the future, we all took credit.

Sight distance was good on the side heading south but shorter heading north due to a curve in the road, so we had to work fast. Keeping an eye out for headlights, we waited until it was dark both ways and hurriedly moved the smudge pots, caution signs, and directional signs to the well-paved area, thereby directing oncoming traffic directly into the hole.

Pleased with our "trick," we hid behind the prickly juniper bushes and watched as car after car followed our misdirected instructions and hit the hole with a thud. Loud expletives followed!

We always referred to this episode as the worst thing we ever did, and it very well may have been. We did not do drugs—skipped that scene altogether. Skipped school one time, got caught but served our time and actually helped the principal in the office. Never stole anything or wrecked the car.

Many times we told this story and neither one of us could remember whether we put the smudge pots and signs back. If not, and you were a victim of this mischief, please accept our sincere apology.

The Wall Came Tumbling Down

Kay lived in a two-story house with her brother, parents, and grandfather. The rooms were big, at least to us at that time, and the family occupied only the first floor. The upstairs was never used, but Kay remembered there were two rooms divided by a wall.

Both of her parents worked, so we tended to hang out at her house when school was not in session. On this particular day, the conversation turned to the upstairs, and since Sandra and I had never been upstairs, we were curious. So we bounded up the stairs to investigate this empty space.

Sure enough, at the top of the stairs there was a door which led to an empty room and beside it was another room, but both were rather small. There was an old couch in one of the rooms along with a headboard and footboard. This was a no-brainer for us. Here we had two unoccupied rooms, and we immediately saw the potential they presented. If we took the wall down, it would make a lovely apartment and a place for lounging (we loved that word—so "movie star-ish"). Most important, it would provide the privacy teenagers yearned for, and at the time we felt we deserved it.

The walls were wood, and now we know it was heart pine, which surely would send the fixer-uppers and renovators out there into convulsions if they knew how we attacked it. Excited and overconfident, we hurried to the garage to accumulate tools and other weapons we might need. Then we rushed back upstairs and began hammering the wall, pulling out nails, and ripping out prized lumber and anything standing in the way of our renovation.

Our intention was to finish the job the same day, before Kay's mother arrived home. It would be nice and neat, much better than before, so surely we would be thanked for our home improvement work.

However, the job was more tedious than expected and quite exhausting. Seems there was something called studs holding this thing up and hundreds of nails attaching the wall to all these studs. Afterward, we would be faced with removing the studs, which were nailed to a board running the length of the wall.

We had, however, developed an efficient method for discarding the lumber. We simply moved the lumber and debris to the top of the stairs and gave it a hard push, which sent it barreling down the stairs into the hall wall, which stopped it instantly. It made a perfect chute. We did not seem to be too concerned about the wall or any person who might amble into our path.

Standing in all the debris, we had just about decided our venture might take more than one day when we heard the back door open and shut. Mrs. Jones came walking through the downstairs hall, gasped as she stepped over the debris, peered up the stairs, and caught a glimpse of our work. Carefully climbing the stairs, she slowly shook her head and quietly said, "What in the world have you girls done?"

Had it been any other parent, I'm sure we would have heard loud yelling, screaming, and doomsday threats, but that was not in Mrs. Jones's character. She was one of the kindest, most humble persons in town. We just stood there, not sure what to do or say. Pathetically, we tried to explain our long-term vision for the project but realized we were not convincing anyone.

We felt obliged to clean as best we could. Then somehow Sandra and I managed to escape, thereby abandoning Kay to deal with her parents.

We were fortunate on this day. Kay's father actually admitted he had been considering doing something about the upstairs and a bit later completed what we had started. However, it was used as a guest bedroom for visiting family members, and we never were able to turn the space into our apartment.

I often think of our determination on that day. Three young girls, devoid of experience, had a vision and firmly set out to accomplish their goal. We also learned another valuable lesson: always check for load-bearing walls!

Thanks for the memory, Sandra.

Postscript: Another time we decided to throw a party and selected Kay's detached garage as the venue. The garage was mainly full of old car parts, engines, tools, and other automotive items. We worked for weeks moving this stuff aside, cleaning oil and gas stains from the cement floor, gathering records for the single playing record player, and fixing food to serve. We tried but never were entirely able to rid the place of the gas smell. We invited our whole class and were pleased with the participation, although to this day, Kay has not forgiven us for again abandoning her when it was time to clean up.

Miles to Go Before We Sleep

Finally, we all reached sixteen years of age, and after completing Tut Burgess's short driving school, we each proudly displayed our driver's license behind the plastic window in our wallet. It was not as difficult back then to obtain a license, although many people would probably still be alive if our generation had required more training. The most challenging task for us was finding a car to use for our road test.

We visited the Highway Patrol office on Highway 70 to take a written test and a short road test. This little office served all of Newton, Hickory, and most of Catawba, but I don't remember it ever being crowded. The only thing we feared was the parallel parking test, which proved a nemesis for many new sixteen-year-olds. The officers were rumored to move the cones depending on a number of things—your manners, good looks, reputation or whether they knew your parents. To this day, one of our young juvenile delinquents, who had been driving his daddy's truck on the back roads since age eleven, swears the cones were inched closer together each time he tried, and eventually the remaining space would not accommodate a bicycle. He finally went to another county to obtain his license.

My brother drove me to the license office in his Buick—the same one that later became subect to vapor locks and left us stranded in the worst places. I passed the written exam and was ushered outside for a short road test and the dreaded parallel parking. I only knocked down one cone, but since I had performed so well on my written exam, the officer issued my license.

Sandra had a little advantage on this occasion. Her father was a policeman in our town, so he drove her to the license office dressed in full uniform. Now we all know that men, and now women, have an unwritten code to accommodate their fellow officers. In fact, Sandra told me once that her father was stopped for excessive speed on the way to Myrtle Beach, but when he informed the officer he was a policeman in his hometown, he was sent on his way with best wishes for a happy holiday. So Sandra passed her written exam and ran all over the cones, but she was still issued a license.

Kay had to wait until her birthday in May, but passed, and we were now all licensed. The problem was that no one had a car.

Getting my brother's car was difficult as he worked and spent weekends with his friends, many of whom did not have cars of their own. Sandra's dad supposedly had experienced too many teenage accidents in his line of work and never allowed Sandra to drive the vehicle unless he accompanied her; not much fun there. Kay's father had a 1957 Ford, but it was almost impossible to be granted permission to drive it.

On one particular Friday or Saturday night, I can't remember which, we were desperate to find a car so we could travel downtown and participate in the long-standing tradition of "bugging the square." Our town was the county seat, and the courthouse set regally on one square block with stores and businesses lining the surrounding streets, which made the square the pulse of our town.

But on weekend nights, it became the favorite hangout, not just for our town but for all the surrounding towns. If you were looking for someone or something to do, you headed for the square. After ball games, dances, or movies, everyone "bugged" the square several times before heading home. It was a chance to catch up with everyone, see who was dating whom, or meet new people.

Only the boys were allowed outside the cars (unwritten rule), so they would park their vehicles in the horizontal spaces, strike their best James Dean pose, and socialize. For a female to stand outside the car was considered "unfit."

We had been unable on this particular weekend night to find transportation to participate in this ritual, and our hearts were aching. It just had to be possible, so we started begging Kay's father for the keys to the Ford. He began with a firm no, but Kay did not let up. She promised everything she could think of until finally she managed to break him down. We promised we would go downtown, park the car, and drive home. Based on this promise, he gave Kay the keys with a strict stipulation: she could go only so many miles. After he checked the odometer, we piled into the car and drove excitedly to the square.

I do not remember the exact mileage we were allowed, but it was low, and we immediately exceeded it. But there were so many people circling the square, our enthusiasm banished the lingering fear we ultimately would have to face. As reality set in, Kay became worried, so we parked at the Dairy Center, a favorite hangout for food, drinks, and curbside service, to plot our alibi.

We considered all the usual excuses, but most of our ideas were fibs which could be quickly checked. Kay dreaded going home, and we were having a hard time coming up with a plausible excuse.

As we were discussing our dilemma, a couple of boys wandered over to our car. These two boys were amateur mechanics and thought of nothing all day except cars and motors. One of them had asked for an engine one year at Christmas, taken it apart, and put it back together. I think he was around twelve at the time. The other sneaked and raced at the drag strip on Sundays—quite well, as he eventually became a NASCAR driver.

The boys suggested we drive the car backward which would reduce the mileage on the vehicle. Well, that made sense! And if anyone knew about these things, it was undoubtedly Jimmy and Morgan. We all agreed it was a good plan.

The Dairy Center crowd was thinning as curfew times approached. The Dairy Center parking lot was adjacent to a large grocery store and accommodated both buildings, which provided a wide berth for circling. We got started. Kay, bless her heart, had to assume the backing up position with her head turned and arm across the back of the seat. Sandra and I watched to make sure the path was clear as well as keeping an eye on the odometer.

Five times around, ten times around, twenty times around—the odometer did not move. We kept going. Kay's neck was sore, we were getting dizzy, and it was late. We couldn't see Jimmy and Morgan; they had left for home as had everyone else at the Dairy Center. We were exasperated, and if we didn't get home soon, there would be more trouble.

After a few more backward passes around the buildings, realizing it was quite late, the rest of us each caught a ride home, leaving Kay at the Dairy Center desperate to get a few miles off that odometer until she finally gave up and went home to face the music. I don't think she ever forgave us for leaving her, and I can't say I blame her.

Kay came out unscathed and even was allowed to drive the car at other times. I guess all of these miscues made her an excellent driver, which we were thankful for one scary Friday night.

It was the same car, the 1957 Ford, and we had it loaded with girls. I was on the passenger side, and Sandra was in the back behind the driver. I'm not sure how many others were on board, but I do know all available spaces were taken. We were breezing along with all the windows rolled down enjoying our evening.

After bugging the square for the umpteenth time, we got involved in a little racing skirmish with some boys. Passing the square, we headed down the street toward the hospital at a speed higher than posted when we encountered a bump in the road. Suddenly, the front hood became unlatched and flew open, blocking our sight. Kay screamed she could not see, put on the brakes and slowed as quickly as possible. There were cars behind us, and we had no idea what was in front. With my head stuck out the right side window and Sandra's out the left side window, we guided Kay to a stopping place so we could close the hood.

It was a scary moment but not the last one we would have in a car.

Good driving, Kay!

Thanks for the memory, Sandra.

Postscript: *I have often wondered if the boys were playing a joke on us or if they genuinely believed backing up would take the miles off. As an adult, I researched this tactic, and it does work (sort of), but we would have had to drive in reverse all the way to Knoxville, Tennessee, and back!*

Fluoride and Bomb Shelters

My grandparents had now moved to Greensboro, where they resided on the conference grounds of the denomination he had served for so many years. Suffering from strokes and now apoplexy, my grandfather could no longer fulfill his duties in the pulpit and needed constant care. He was a pioneer in this conference, having started several churches and rescued others from closing their doors. Out of respect, the church conference had very kindly moved them into an apartment in the conference facility where my grandmother could look after him. In exchange for housing and a small stipend, all the church asked was their presence and light maintenance on the grounds year around.

As always, as soon as school ended, my sister and I journeyed to our grandparents' home, wherever home was at that time, for an extended visit. The Greensboro location was a favorite of ours as we had the run of the grounds, which had several dormitories, a large tabernacle where we could play church, ball fields, and many trails and dirt roads for biking.

During the 1950s there were no cell phones, and long distance calls were reserved for emergencies due to the cost. Therefore, Sandra and I had no communication during this time, so when I returned home, we were excited to see each other and spent the next several days catching up.

After she related all the news happening in the neighborhood, I had only one question for her. "Have they put fluoride in the water in Newton?" She looked puzzled.

Either Sandra had not listened to the radio since I was away, or the newscasters in Newton just were not up to speed. My grandmother turned on the radio every hour to get the news and other times for call-in talk shows—every morning and afternoon—and this year they had plenty to discuss.

Our country was at the height of the Cold War, which had everyone expecting a bomb to come cruising out of the sky and wipe out the entire population suddenly and without warning. Now, in addition, the powers that be were adding fluoride to the drinking water in hopes of preventing or at least lessening tooth decay, especially in children. When I communicated this to Sandra, she thought it was a good idea.

Well, so had I at first, but after educating myself by listening to the talk shows, I had developed grave concerns. Many people had become convinced that this was a plot by the Russians to slowly annihilate the youth of America by deteriorating their brains; as the aging population died off, the Communists would take over. I had heard this twice every day since I had been gone and was quite terrified.

Greensboro had decided to add fluoride to the drinking water, so those in charge must be Communists, according to the callers. Each day the same callers dialed the show citing a variety of statistics, real or made up, supporting their claims. I was not mature enough to realize the medical professionals and scientists had been studying this concept for years, compiling endless amounts of scientific data, and recommended this action after extensive research. As I learned later, the callers had endless time on their hands and nothing better to do than promote conspiracy theories. Call-in talk shows sometimes bring out the worst in our population. Conversely, the professionals could not call in and dispute these theories; they were busy working and saving lives.

My grandmother knew the truth, but she had no idea I was becoming alarmed, so she failed to put my mind at ease. Therefore, my anxiety persisted, and now that I had returned home and shared my concerns with Sandra, she was also alarmed.

As our distress grew, so did our compulsion to save the world, which for us was Newton. We theorized that Greensboro was a much larger city, and perhaps the news had just not traveled our way. Before our town decided to dump this poison in our water, we felt it was our duty to sound the alarm. So we set about devising our plan.

The most obvious choice for delivering this message was the radio. We had a radio station in Newton with a loyal base, thanks to the entrepreneurial spirit of its owner. Our station did not have a dedicated theme but made an effort to satisfy everyone's interest. On Sunday, there was gospel singing, and local preachers conducted services at the station. Nights—especially weekends—there was rock 'n' roll presented by a DJ who was quite popular. We knew him well; his parents lived in our neighborhood, and his wife and children attended our church, though we never saw him there.

On Friday nights, the station broadcast a play-by-play of our high school football team as well as the Twins baseball games, a minor league team that descended on our town each summer. At noon, an organ rendition of "Sweet Hour of Prayer" played while a somber announcer read the obituaries followed by a popular show on the station, *The Swap Shop*. People would call the station and offer their used possessions for sale or to swap for another item. No one hesitated to give their phone number and address and say when they would be home. There was news every hour, with plenty of local commercials, and most importantly, before sign-off each evening, "The Star Spangled Banner" was played. As teenagers, this was how we knew we had missed curfew.

But the most popular figure at the station was the owner, Earl Holder, who had invented a character named Grandpappy Millsaps. Pappy was probably the most loved human being in our town. Mr. Holder would dress the part in overalls, glasses, straw hat, and a distinctive country drawl. He promoted the local downtown merchants on Saturday by standing in the back of a truck with a microphone and announcing winners for merchant drawings and always pushing the local businesses. One thing was for sure: Mr. Holder loved this town.

His most famous program came on weekdays each morning, the *Silver Dollar Hour*. I wish I knew more about the history of how Mr. Holder came up with this compelling idea. Every homemaker was glued to the radio for one hour that morning. Offices and factories would allow workers to tune into the radio during this time, and every truck and car radio turned their dial to WNNC. Even administrative offices at the schools tuned in.

Mr. Holder would read a question. It was never a simple question, but it also was not a complicated math problem. It just required some research, and without the internet, this might mean a trip to the library. The program had a distinct cash register sound to call people's attention, and Mr. Holder would announce with enthusiasm, "Welcome to the *Silver Dollar Hour!*" He would call someone randomly chosen from the phone book. If there was an answer, he asked the question, and if they answered correctly, they received all the silver dollars in the till. Otherwise, another silver dollar was added to the till, which continued to grow until the answer was correctly given.

This program utterly consumed our entire town. When a new question was read, party lines were tied up by listeners searching for the answer. The question was repeated and discussed in every barber and beauty shop, local cafes, stores, courtrooms, businesses, and schools. Some teachers would even include the questions in homework assignments. Once a person correctly answered the question, this process started anew.

So it became apparent to Sandra and me that we needed to get our message out via our local radio station—but how?

At this time we were shy of our early teens and easily influenced by adults and their opinions. But in Greensboro, they had said it on the radio, so it must be true. After much thought, we decided our best option was to write a letter to Mr. Holder warning him of the imminent risk and ask him to alert the citizens of Newton on the air, preferably during the *Silver Dollar Hour*. We could think of no one who had more clout or respect than Mr. Holder. Plus, he had a radio station!

We labored over the letter for a full day, making sure nothing was omitted. I was full of knowledge from the airwaves in Greensboro and had heard plenty about the Communists in Russia and their desire to take over the world. They were behind us in developing atomic weapons, so seizing the opportunity to infiltrate our water supply was a good alternative. Many of our elected officials were involved in this plot, so Mr. Holder should first alert the public before discussing with those in power. The letter was a full two pages but very detailed and specific as to how he should approach the problem.

Retrieving an envelope and stamp from my mother's sewing machine drawer, we addressed the envelope and walked to Dude Dellinger's store where a green mailbox was located. Mailboxes had not yet been painted blue but were a drab Army green. Then we waited and waited and waited.

We tried to stay close to the radio, especially when Mr. Holder was on the air. Surely, he would view this as urgent and most likely would read the letter first during the *Silver Dollar Hour*. When we missed the broadcast, we would always ask our mothers, "Did Mr. Holder mention anything about fluoride in the water?" They just stared at us bewildered or shooed us away.

Our concern did not weaken. In fact, the Cold War was heating up, and a sense of fear overcame the population. Church prayers always included a prayer to deliver us from the Communist threat and guide us in the right direction. There was an assortment of pamphlets published and distributed through the mail, waiting rooms and businesses on how to prepare for and survive a nuclear attack. The safest and best answer was a bomb shelter.

These pamphlets carefully described how to turn a cellar or basement into a safe bomb shelter and encouraged all new home builders to include a shelter in their homes. A national program was initiated designating existing buildings as fallout shelters, as it was believed these shelters would protect one from falling particles. Fallout shelters were recognizable by a large yellow and black sign so people could find one closest to them. The basement of the Catawba County Courthouse on the square was the one Sandra and I decided we would make a run for, since it was large, was made of concrete, and had a drink machine.

But there was a builder (or a family) close to our neighborhood who decided a bomb shelter would be best if incorporated into new construction. So they included a bomb shelter into their new home plans which were being constructed past Two Joe Hill. We were excited to hear this.

We watched progress on the home when we were in the area, but it was slow. We were never present when the shelter was being constructed, but friends close by described it to us in full detail. It had rows of shelves holding years of canned food, water to last for ages, batteries for flashlights, soap, clothing, etc. Over the years the house became known as "the house with a bomb shelter" and was an attraction for Sunday afternoon drives as well as visitors.

We never heard back from Mr. Holder, and as we grew older and matured intellectually, we were somewhat embarrassed by our deed. We hoped he would not remember our names, especially during another encounter with him during our high school years.

Sometime around our freshman or sophomore year in high school, we were presented with our first opportunity to skip classes. Before hearing our classmates boast of their experiences skipping school, we had not considered such an adventure. We were intrigued, and one day our conscience took a turn for the worse when the perfect opening presented itself.

For some reason, I cannot remember why, Sandra's parents went out-of-town for the day—probably a funeral. Supposedly, Sandra and her sister would be in school, and her parents would return before nightfall. Realizing we would have the house to ourselves for the day, we put our plan in place.

We shared our intentions, with a classmate who willingly offered to write our excuses which we both presented to our individual homeroom teachers. Both notes explained there was a death in the family, and we needed to attend out-of-town funerals. Each was signed with our mother's name—in entirely different handwriting from all the other documents in our file.

On the day of execution, we rose, dressed, gathered our books and met at our regular meeting place to catch the bus but instead, cut through the field, hoping to go unnoticed and surreptitiously crept into Sandra's house.

After helping ourselves to the remaining pound cake and watching morning TV shows, we turned the radio to a Charlotte station and were earnestly practicing our shag steps to "60 Minute Man" when the telephone rang. We were teenagers who spent a great deal of time hoping for the phone to ring, so Sandra lunged for the receiver without thinking and in her best soft, demure voice said, "Hello." It went something like this:

"Well, good morning! Who is speaking?"

"This is Sandra."

"Well, Sandra, is your mother or father there? This is the *Silver Dollar Hour* calling."

"No, they are both out-of-town."

"So you are there by yourself?

"No, my friend Phyllis is here with me."

"Where do you girls go to school?"

"Newton-Conover High."

"Well, Sandra, shouldn't you be in school?"

It occurred to both of us at the same time! The whole town was listening to this broadcast including the principal's office! Sandra carefully placed the receiver back in its cradle.

Thanks for the memory, Sandra.

Postscript: The WNNC radio station is still in existence, and when I am in the area, I always tune in. Somehow it is soothing. Mr. Holder has passed away, but the memory of Grandpappy Millsaps will always be with us. Much of the town's population is now too young to remember him, but for those who do, it brings a smile.

We did not get in trouble at school for this mishap, but the busybodies in our neighborhood raced to be the first to report us to our parents.

I love going by "the house with the bomb shelter" and pointing it out to family members. I wonder if they have turned it into a man cave or an exercise room.

Sexual Harassment – We Got This!

There were some plusses (and minuses) to being born during WWII. A big plus was that we missed the drug scene entirely. By the mid to late 1960s, we were married, figuring out budgets, starting families, and chasing children. We did catch the women's revolution, which mainly meant we went to work and became experts at running a household and parenting, while holding down a steady job.

We also missed the sexual revolution and free love phase our counterparts enjoyed. Sex education for Sandra and me was pieced together by eavesdropping on adult conversations, discussions with our friends, and sneaking a peek at wildly illustrated books while avoiding the watchful eye of the librarian. And of course, our incident with Junior and Fannie, as related previously.

Our parents avoided the subject entirely, hoping we would never learn of such a thing as sex, which left formal sex education to Ms. Gettys at school. Ms. Gettys was our health and physical education teacher and coach of the girls' high school basketball team. The fact that she never married puzzled us as to why she was chosen for our sex education; we were under the impression sex was not allowed until one was united in marriage. That is, the girl was not allowed; it seemed this did not apply to the boys, although that would not seem possible if the female population adhered to their rule.

Sometime during the year, Ms. Gettys would set aside a few

hours to teach us what she felt we needed to know about the birds and the bees and then show a film. It left all the girls red-faced, and I don't know what it did to the boys as they were separated from us. The lesson consisted of a diagram of a boy's and a girl's body. We were taught the proper names for the body parts and how the bodies engaged, resulting in the production of a baby. The diagrams were quite plain with a slit for the female sex organ and a little loop for the male sex organ. Ms. Gettys never asked if anyone had a question, and there was no pop quiz.

But somehow Sandra and I figured all this out and went about being teenagers. It was the norm for boys (and men) to whistle at girls, make comments, and so on. Harassment rules had not been established yet, and we chose to enjoy or dislike the attention based on the age, looks, and character of the giver. It was all we knew to do.

It was summertime, and each day, after our necessary chores at home were completed, we set about finding a ride to the river. The river was our favorite summer hangout. There were several choice river locations, but our favorite was Sunset Beach about ten miles away. There was a cleared area with sand and a pier where boats could dock, and it was free. I do not remember any of the swimming areas located along the rivers charging a fee to swim or even park. We had a local community pool in town that charged an entrance fee and one outside of town which we frequented sometimes, but mostly we hung out at the free ones.

Unable to secure a ride on this particular day, we decided to "borrow" my brother's car, drive to the river and return before the 5:00 whistle blew. My brother worked at Broyhill Furniture a few blocks from home. Because it was so close, and he was extremely tight with his money, Jimmy chose to walk to work most days. The car was a 1953 Buick, which had a proclivity to vapor-lock during hot weather. Most likely this was due to an improvised air conditioner that had been added to the car by an amateur. It never worked, and no one could figure out how to remove it.

For no explainable reason, once the car ran for a while during hot weather, it would just stop and refuse to restart until the engine was cool again. Numerous mechanics had worked on the car, and charged well, but none had ever been able to correct this problem. Driving during the summer was challenging, but we decided to take a chance.

It was about a quarter mile from my house to Main Street which would lead us to the road heading toward Sunset Beach. As we neared the corner of Main Street, the Buick vapor-locked and stopped in place. Concerned we would be seen by someone who knew us and relay our predicament to Jimmy, I put the car in neutral while Sandra pushed us behind a private garage that housed a local race car driver's car. (This driver went on to become a well-known NASCAR driver, as did his son, but this was during the early stages of his career, well before state-of-the-art facilities and full-time staff were affordable. In fact, the chief mechanic worked at the local Ford dealership during the day and worked on the race car at night. The crew was always pleasant to the local kids and would let us hang out.)

We sat for what seemed like hours, trying periodically to start that old Buick, until finally, it cranked. Still determined to make it to the river, we eased onto the road only to hear a *thump, thump, thump* and feel the right front of the car drop dramatically. It seemed we had picked up a nail in the race car garage or driveway.

Thankfully, in front of the garage on the corner of Main Street was a service station with a bay for mechanical work. We coasted into the service station, asked the cost to patch a tire, and searched through our belongings and the car seats until we could cover the cost. By now, we knew we were not going to make it to the river, so we sat down in the little service station office in front of the fan while our tire was being fixed. Our new goal was to make it back home before Jimmy got off work.

It was a dirty, smelly office filled with overflowing cigarette ashtrays. The windows covering two sides of the office were so dirty, it was difficult to see outside clearly. The floor was bare cement stained with years of grease, dirt, and oil. A grimy pay phone hung on the wall next to the door leading to the bay area. We had heard someone was shot through the window while talking on the phone so we slid our chairs down next to the cigarette machine.

The counter, covered with a sheet of glass, was in as bad shape as the floor. Under the glass were pictures of pin-up girls, phone numbers, and business cards of tow trucks and other vendors. On the wall was a calendar from Saunders Furniture Store in Conover, the same one that hung in both our kitchens.

We could hear the banging in the bay as the hubcap was tossed aside, and nuts and caps thrown into it for safekeeping. The rim was set aside and the tire placed on the holder for patching. We assumed the silence was because the patching was quiet; then came the same sounds again, only in reverse. At last, the jack came down, and hopefully we were done.

The mechanic called, "You girls git back here!"

Relieved we were close to escaping this unhealthy environment, we hurriedly walked to the bay area and suddenly found ourselves cornered in the back of the bay next to a long cabinet strewn with tools. The car sat a few feet from us, but blocking our path was the burly mechanic. His black hair was curly and matted against his head from sweat, which also dripped from his forehead and his bushy eyebrows. He had removed his shirt exposing his hairy chest and arms. There was an unidentifiable tattoo on each bicep. He smelled of grease, oil, and dirty sweat. All of a sudden we were terrified.

He started toward us, forcing us to back against the counter. In a surly voice, with a sheepish grin on his face, he asked, "And now what do you girls like to do for fun?"

I'm sure the frightened look on our faces only encouraged him as he crept nearer. Neither of us answered, but both were thinking the same thing: *This is how we are going to die.* As our heads turned toward each other, I glanced down at the counter; Sandra did the same. Reading each other's minds, as we did all our lives, we dropped into survival mode. I picked up a greasy lug wrench, and she picked up the crowbar. We could feel ourselves filling with power as we raised them above our heads.

Our attacker looked startled and cried out, "Now girls, girls— no need for that." He was backing up as we stepped toward him. In truth, we were trying to get to the car, but when he began running, a chase ensued. The bathrooms were outside, and he reached the men's restroom and locked the door just in time. Now we were emboldened and felt obligated to take this one step further for the sake of our fellow females and pave the way for others in the future. (We added that part later on.)

We banged our weapons on the door while he yelled for us to get off the premises. Slowly, our courage began to weaken and reality set in. Also, customers from the Midway Diner next door were staring. So we jumped in that old Buick, praying all the while for it to start. We raced home, parked the car, and were sitting on the front porch when Jimmy arrived home. As he passed by the Buick, he reached out his hand for an obligatory pat on the hood. Unfortunately for us, the engine had not yet cooled.

Thanks for the memory, Sandra.

Postscript: *This is the first of many incidents I could relate where we encountered harassment or abuse. Times were different, much different, and the environment was not in our favor. Most of these incidents we did not divulge to others but often discussed between ourselves, expressing outrage but determined to do our part. Once, an adult male blatantly groped us in a crowded Eagles Dime Store. When we mentioned the episode to the floorwalker (a manager assigned to walking the floor), we were met with scorn. A mailman assigned to our neighborhood made numerous attempts to enter our homes if he could tell an adult was not present. We learned to lock the screen door and hide under the bed if we were alone.*

Neither of us held political offices, organized or led marches, but we voted religiously and supported those we felt were sympathetic to women's rights and abuse. We both were blessed with daughters whose lives and professions hopefully have benefitted from change and progress. But there is still much to do.

Jimmy was not too happy with us, but he didn't stay mad long. He later was drafted into the army and, after discharge, returned to Broyhill Furniture, where he worked until his early death.

The First Taste of Beer

S andra and I spent a lot of time on our front porches, as did most people during our era. Porches were a method of communication, learning, and watchfulness as well as an excellent security system. Between bouts of laundry, cooking, and cleaning, a housewife would spend her breaks on the front porch with a glass of tea rather than in front of a TV. Porches gave one a glimpse of what was going on in the neighborhood, let one wave to passing cars, and offered the pure enjoyment of a cool summer breeze.

We both had nice front porches, but I now lived on a more traveled road which meant more cars with more boys and more activity to engage our interest. My porch wrapped around the front and side of our house. The front steps were bordered on both sides by a brick wall with a cement cap giving each of us an ideal place to pose nonchalantly with an uninvolved "cool" look as each car rounded the curve.

In those days, there were fewer makes of cars (nothing foreign mind you), and they were immediately identifiable by their grills and hood ornaments. Vehicles in the 1950s had personalities and character, and we gravitated toward our favorites. By the age of twelve, every child knew the make, model, and year of all cars mainly due to the Name That Car game. Players would line up in the yard so each had the same view when a car came into sight. The person who named the model and year first for the most cars was the winner.

Due to this attained knowledge, we knew what everyone drove and whether or not an approaching car was worth striking our best pose or, even more significant, making eye contact.

We also learned much about our neighbors and their habits—and for one particular household, when the fighting would begin. One married couple fought about everything, and even though they stayed married until death did them part, I don't think they ever agreed on anything except their love for a good argument.

Almost everyone in the neighborhood worked in one of the mills. Newton was not a one-mill town; we had many small mills and several quite large plants, mainly textiles. In my neighborhood, Broyhill Furniture was located just several blocks north. It was a good size plant—so big, in fact, that a small store was located directly across the street to provide lunch and snacks for the employees. We never entered this store. I'm sure it was open to the public, but we just assumed it was meant only for the plant workers; hence its nickname, the plant store.

For those readers who were not raised in a mill town, the mills felt it was their obligation to also act as a clock for the neighborhood and nearby workers. Therefore, an ear-shattering whistle would blow five minutes before starting time and again at starting time to draw attention to the latecomers. The same happened again at noon, signaling lunch, and at quitting time. And to make sure the entire town did not lose track of time, the fire station set off a siren blast at noon each day.

In retrospect, this was a beneficial service provided to the community. Children knew when to head home for lunch and supper. When the five o'clock whistle blew, wives began scooping up dinner from the stove so that when the tired and weary workers arrived home, they could head directly to the table for a hot meal.

Sandra and I grew up surrounded by all of this, but we also noticed from our front porch lookout something a little different on Fridays. Some workers owned cars, which were always full of carpoolers, but many in the neighborhood walked to work. During the week, when the five o'clock whistle sounded, the men would walk across to the plant store and pick up a carton of Pepsi-Colas. Tired, smelling of shellac, and covered with dust, they walked with heads down drudgingly lugging their cartons of Pepsis. After dinner, each of them settled on the front porch, a Pepsi in hand, and waited for the sun to go down and the evening breeze to bring relief.

But on Friday, it was different. They didn't stop by the plant store but instead visited another store a little off their regular route. It took them longer, but they walked faster, a spring in their step, their head up, eyes forward and swinging a six pack of *beer*. Sometimes they even waved at us!

So we became curious. What was it about this mysterious thing called beer? There was an age limit on purchasing the brew, and preachers railed about it in the pulpit, referring to it as the drink of the devil. Still, people would spend their last dime for a bottle or can, risking ridicule, and for heaven's sake, you were not even allowed to drive when you drank it! Was it that tantalizing?

We could only assume the taste was so incredible, certainly better than a Pepsi-Cola, the best beverage to have ever touched our lips, that a person must be an adult to handle the excitement. Many at our school had not been able to wait until they reached the appropriate age and had sneaked a purchase or raided their parents' stash. They spoke of these episodes with intrigue and braggadocio. We couldn't wait!

By now we were in high school and had welcomed another friend into our fold, Pat. Pat was tall, blond, and destined to become a model. She had beautiful skin, and her regal walk always turned heads. Pat brought with her an unmatched sense of humor and a sophisticated approach to life. I always said, and told her many times, as soon as she realized Newton had a city limit, she began to figure out a way to get past it.

If there was a party within twenty-five miles, Pat knew about it. She could spot a tall, good-looking man from a distance in a crowded room. Ambitious, she was always seeking the next level. Why spend time on immature high school boys when a college was just fifteen miles up the road? Hence, Pat got wind of and finagled an invitation to a fraternity party on campus at Lenoir-Rhyne College (now a university), and they were going to have *beer*.

This event warranted some planning. Parents must not know, but that was easy. We were good kids, so they would believe we were going to a school dance. However, we might be arriving home late, so Pat decided we would have a pajama party in her basement and likewise informed her parents we would come in through the outside basement door so as not to disturb them. We would be quiet, with no loud music or talking, as the next day was Sunday, and we all had to go to church. That made them proud. Pat just had a way with words.

Our excitement grew with each passing moment. We had transportation in place, were pretty sure we knew where to go, and had worked on our wardrobe (stepped up a little to a college level), and for sure we were college kids, perhaps visiting from Appalachian State Teachers College (later became a university), or one of the other nearby colleges. Mainly, we were consumed with just how this beverage would taste. The foamy, bubbly part must be the best tasting. Should we shake it up first, or would it naturally form bubbles? The excitement kept growing.

It was easy to find the fraternity house, identifiable by hundreds of students converging, spilling out across the yard, and sprawling atop cars. The lawn was crowded to the last square inch. We walked bravely up the stairs, following Pat's lead, trying to stand up straight and mimic her model's walk. She moved as if she had been there before and spoke to others, smiling and laughing like an adult until she found us a suitable niche surrounded by frat brothers and coeds.

Stacked on the counter were rows of Country Club beer ideally packaged in small cans deemed fashionable for women, who were also inspired by the name. Country Club beer was a malt liquor with a high alcohol content, which today makes me question the marketing ethics of those distilleries. We were encouraged to help ourselves which we promptly did, trying to hide the fact that we were novices. With the beer open, we settled back, raised our cans, and together took our first big gulp of the worst-tasting liquid that had ever touched our lips!

We stared at each other in horror. Our disappointment was obvious, but our new friends were encouraging. They advised us to drink slowly and let our taste buds get used to the unique taste. "It may take a while," they said, "but stay with it." We honestly gave it that old college try, but it never got better.

How we wished drinking this horrible brew was the worst that could happen, and it was for that night. The next morning was when it got worse. Our heads pounded, and our stomachs refused to accept any food after rejecting what was already there. Our mouths felt as if we had been licking ashtrays all night. It took us all day to begin feeling human again.

After that experience, we determined one thing for sure: beer never would taste as good as a Pepsi-Cola, let alone a milkshake from the Dairy Center. We also had our doubts that all the braggadocio by the boys was only hype.

Thanks for the memory, Sandra.

Postscript: *Pat did go on to do some modeling and always stayed true to her free spirit. None of us ever became drinkers except for a glass of wine here or there. We all decided this potent stuff simply was not worth the aftermath.*

Left to right: Sandra, Phyllis, Pat, Kay

We Love a Parade

Throughout our adult lives, Sandra, Pat, Kay, and I maintained a friendship, although at times distance presented a challenge. Pat spent most of her adult life in Philadelphia but returned to Newton in the mid-1990s. It is a place that draws you home, thanks to the many memories. I was only an hour away, and Sandra and Kay resided in the area.

A common denominator for our celebrations was the Old Soldiers Reunion held the third week in August, honoring soldiers past and present. It is one of oldest continuous reunions of this type in the country. The event is highly anticipated by all ages and engages the entire county. As young children, we looked forward to the rides, vendors with cotton candy, beauty pageants, dog parades, cakewalks, music, and of course, the climatic end – the five o'clock parade on Thursday afternoon.

Leading up to the parade are nightly concerts on the square including gospel singing, big band, bluegrass, and beach music. Beauty pageants are held throughout the week, with the winners taking their positions on one of the floats retrieved from storage. Newton did not mess around with these pageants. It was a big deal to be Miss Reunion, and we were all rooting for our favorites.

However, our town did not settle for just one queen. We crowned a Baby Miss Reunion, a Tiny Miss Reunion, a Little Miss Reunion, a Junior Miss Reunion, a Teen Miss Reunion, a Miss Reunion (that was the big one), and later a Ms. Reunion for those twenty-three and older. These beauties were placed on floats and driven up and down College and Main Streets, which formed the two-hour parade route.

In addition, beauty queens from all the surrounding high schools were placed on floats or in the backseats of convertibles. Bands from the neighboring high schools marched and played their school songs, and politicians rode in cars, preferably convertibles with poster board signs taped on the sides, to greet their constituents. Cannons roared, rifles were fired, clowns threw candy, and businesses promoted themselves on floats, trailers, or newly washed and waxed autos.

As adults, we decided this reunion was the perfect time for us to descend on our hometown and partake in the events. Although we might miss a night or two of concerts, depending on the genre, we all congregated on Thursday, the finale, for the parade.

Reuniting with old friends we had not seen since our school years, brushing up on our shag steps, and finding unique items from the multitude of vendors brought much joy and sustained us for the coming year. We reserved our place on the square by placing our chairs on the street early, sometimes gaining a spot on the steps of a reserved platform.

We freely offered our critique and after several years decided it was getting a little boring. It seems there were too many trucks, cars, and other nonchalant vehicles just driving through. In fact, once a large tractor-trailer without writing or emblems anywhere on the cab was slowly making its way through the parade route. Someone asked him who or what he was representing, and he countered he had taken a wrong turn off Highway 16 and wound up in the parade. This parade definitely needed our input.

So after a few years of pondering this issue, Pat suddenly had an idea; at first we did not embrace it. Kay's husband, Kermit, was a big fan of John Deere equipment and owned several collectibles and refurbished tractors. He participated in many John Deere events throughout the state and always drove a tractor in the Soldiers Reunion Parade. He would hitch a large trailer behind the tractor, and his church would drape a banner on the sides. A few members would climb on board and ride in the parade promoting the church.

This particular year, the church decided not to participate, so Kermit offered that anyone who wanted to jump on board was welcome. Pat seized the opportunity, Kay was lukewarm, and Sandra and I said *no*. As daring as we had been growing up, the idea of riding behind this tractor with the entire town staring at us was not appealing.

But Pat persisted, so discussions began. We needed a theme. Ideas were presented and all rejected. However, a tractor reminded us of farming, the country, and such, so it seemed only fitting to let the tractor guide us toward a theme. A Hawaiian or New York theme just didn't make sense on a tractor. So the winner was *Hee Haw*!

Preparations began immediately. Kay was a talented artist, so the job of replicating the *Hee Haw* donkey fell to her; we needed two, one for each side. Crepe paper, hay, wood boxes, corn stalks—all of this we gathered for decorating. We obtained straw hats, jeans, overalls, bandanas, shirts, and anything else reminiscent of *Hee Haw*. We confiscated a boom box and a bluegrass tape to play on the parade route.

We would all arrive early at Pat's home, where Alison, her daughter, a talented esthetician, would give us pigtails, freckles, and missing teeth. Fortunately, Pat lived only a couple blocks from the parade assembly grounds, so we could walk to our destination.

Plans were made to meet the Sunday before to decorate the trailer in Kermit's warehouse. The finished product was excellent, with the donkeys, corncobs, cornstalks, and hay promoting our theme. But it became exceptional once we added the final finishing touch: an old toilet, tastefully decorated in Hee Haw fashion, designated as the "outhouse" and placed in the middle of our float.

It was hot on parade day, but we were exuberant. Along the way, Sandra and I had overcome our doubts about being exposed to the world with less than flattering makeup and clothes and now were eager to get going. Alison did a fantastic job on our makeup, and we actually looked cute. We had never clogged before, but somehow, on that trailer with bluegrass music blasting, it came naturally.

We pulled out of the parade assembly grounds with music blaring, our cowbells ringing, and a few clogging steps. Our entry was toward the parade end, due to the noise of the tractor, so when we arrived at the heart of the parade route, the crowd was tiring from endless floats, cars, and trucks. We were an immediate hit, which encouraged our antics more. Since it was hot, we drank continuously from our jugs to stay hydrated and energized.

All this liquid may not have been a good idea for women slightly past middle age with shrinking bladders. Pat was the first to cave and announced she could not wait any longer and had to use the outhouse on the float. We were aghast, but she insisted.

Quickly, we gathered materials being used for other purposes and created a makeshift cover around the commode. We were barely able to shelter Pat from the waist down so she would have to navigate and improvise the rest. Concerned only about her bloated bladder, she called on her modeling background and slid gracefully onto the commode, all the while maintaining her dignity, smiling and waving at the crowd. With sleight of hand she nimbly managed to lower her overalls and settle like a beauty queen on an out-of-sight would-be throne, emptying her bladder while smiling and waving to the crowd the whole time. No one, except those on board, had any idea she was engaging in an act of nature.

Unfortunately, the selection committee had already handed out the award for the best float before we arrived at the parade end. Additionally, we were informed that our trailer pulled by a tractor did not meet the criteria of a "float."

Thanks for the memory, Sandra.

Postscript: *As of this writing, the Soldiers Reunion is over 130 years old and believed to be the oldest running patriotic celebration in the United States. At one time, our male residents would grow beards in tribute, but alas, that ritual has passed. The merchants still display memorabilia and old pictures in their windows. The American flag is draped on every storefront, flown from every pole, displayed in yards, and waved by attendees. Vendors return each year along with new ones, businesses close for the celebration, and the parade still lasts for hours.*

As students, we marched in the parade as cheerleaders and band members. It was tiring, always hot, but we were delighted to be on display and hear the cheers from the crowd. The Reunion committee works hard to prepare for this event, which drives business to the merchants, denotes that summer will soon end, school will begin and provides a venue for old friends to come together. Should you be in the area the third week of August, the city of Newton will welcome you.

Top: Kay, Sandra
Bottom: Phyllis, Pat

Senior Prom for Seniors

Turning sixty can affect people differently. Realizing there is more sand in the bottom of the hourglass than the top can be depressing, while others celebrate that retirement is nearing. Conversely, some pay little attention to this milestone.

For Sandra, Pat, Kay, and me, it was none of the above. In fact, one might make a good case that we reverted to our second childhood and were overtaken by sheer silliness. I prefer to think it was a decade of heightened ingenuity on our part.

It all began with my birthday one April when we reached our mid-sixties. Up until that day, we treated birthdays like normal people—with cards (funny and serious) and lunch or dinner. So I was pleased when Sandra and Pat decided to drive to Charlotte for my birthday, have lunch, and do some shopping. (I'm not sure where Kay was; most likely at the beach.)

They acted weird immediately upon arrival. Both were sporting funky, brightly colored sunglasses that obviously offered no sun protection and would have been more suitable on a nine-year-old. They hurried through lunch, exchanging secret glances, speaking in a language of innuendos, and unable to wipe that sheepish grin from their faces.

I was truly puzzled and concerned something had gone awry, but once I saw the armful of presents they were toting, I forgot any apprehension and was delirious with joy. All for me! Yes, they assured me, every single one was for me, so I jumped right in.

The presents were expertly wrapped with gorgeous bows waiting to reveal a surely coveted gift. The first one, in sparkly paper with a huge bow, was hiding a roll of toilet paper. *What? It must be part of a puzzle*, so I kept going. The second one, with the delightful pompom ribbon, held a pack of thumbtacks. I continued removing the elegant wrappings from the disappointing contents until I finally reached the legitimate gift.

I cannot remember what the nice gift was. I just remember the toilet paper, nails, glue, toilet bowl brush, silly sunglasses, and other types of miscellany. But I knew that day Sandra and Pat had started something. From now on, birthdays would never be the same. I also resolved, and warned them, that a huge payback was in their future.

Our silliness continued, but lingering in the back of my mind was a plan I shared with the others for a very special birthday surprise for Sandra.

Our high school held many dances during our time: homecoming, sock hops, Sadie Hawkins, and the biggest of all, the junior and senior proms. It's refreshing that even today the senior prom is considered a grand occasion and approached with the same enthusiasm as in past generations. It is the most formal high school affair and, for most, the first time curfews are lifted. Of course, ours were held in the school gym, whereas now many rent an event site.

Some of our most memorable times happened at these dances, especially the proms. As we reminisced about the fun times later in life, Sandra constantly reminded us of one fact that she just could not let go of. She never owned a prom dress.

Somehow I had managed a prom dress for both proms by using the layaway plan. Kay, always the best dressed with inroads to the best fashion shop in town, was well taken care of, and Pat, a beauty pageant contestant, seemed to have a closet full of gowns. Sandra, for whatever reason, just borrowed from these collections, and no one paid particular attention, as she could wear any color and any style and always look great.

But through the years, without warning, Sandra would suddenly lament, "You know I never owned a prom dress." I never knew how to respond to this statement or what to do to relieve her anxiety. So on her sixty-fifth (or thereabouts) birthday, we decided to end the drama and set about reconstructing and reenacting our senior prom to put this issue to rest.

Pat was confident she remembered the theme, "A Night of Fantasy," along with a good idea of the decorations. We had to have the traditional punchbowl surrounded by sugar cookies, balloons, and crepe paper bunting twisted and draped across the ceiling. A throne, tiara, and bouquet awaited our new prom queen, which for sure would be Sandra.

We set about preparing for this event with the same enthusiasm we felt almost fifty years before. We assigned different chores, coordinated our preparation and decorating times, and set a date for the big event. Pat's childhood home was vacant, and she kindly offered the residence as our venue.

We prepared Sandra by explaining we had come up with a special night but could not share the details. We would take care of everything, so "Be home waiting for our arrival on the designated night. Just be sure to wear clean underwear," to which she exclaimed, "I am *not* wearing a bathing suit anywhere!"

Kay already had decided on her attire, so Pat and I scoured the local Goodwill and secondhand stores for prom dresses suitable for us and Sandra. This was not an easy task, as evening dresses today are much more provocative and not suitable for women in their sixties. But finally we succeeded, and the big day arrived.

We were as secretive as possible explaining only to her family that something big was taking place, and they would probably enjoy watching. They just had to hide until we arrived and make sure Sandra did not leave the house.

The funeral home where Sandra worked part-time graciously agreed to provide a limousine after Kay informed the owner of our surprise. We would dress at the prom venue; then the limousine would pick us up and drive us to Sandra's, where we would dress her in her *own* prom dress, blindfold her, and take her to the prom.

Little did we know the police had been informed of our little escapade, so we were surprised but pleased when a patrol car was waiting for us at the city limits to escort us to Sandra's house. We arrived with sirens blaring and lights flashing; neighbors and hidden family members converged on the scene. Sandra confided later she was mortified and very much concerned as to what we had concocted.

We read a declaration stating our concern that this nemesis of never owning a prom dress was out of hand. But no worries: we had conjured up a plan to enable her to overcome her affliction. This would be her night, and "By all means, keep the prom dress—it's yours!" Then we went about the task of dressing her (hence the clean underwear), applying makeup and glitter, and blindfolded her for the trip to the prom.

When we arrived, Pat led a blindfolded Sandra into the house, where she removed the blindfold and we all welcomed her to the prom. Using the same theme, the room was easily recognizable as a replica of the original senior prom held in our old high school gym. We had managed the surprise, and she was overwhelmed!

Relying on our memories, we conducted this evening as closely as we could to the actual ritual almost a half-century earlier. We formally announced special songs from the fifties as if a live band was present. The processional was quite elegant as we presented ourselves to the court.

Finally, it was time for the coronation ceremony. We each waited under pretense in anticipation as names were called for the titles of Miss Congeniality, Second Runner-Up, and, next to the top prize, First Runner-Up.

The importance of the First Runner-Up was carefully explained by Pat. "The First Runner-Up has a special duty to the crown. If for any reason the queen cannot fulfill her duties, such as an illness or getting married, pregnant, or convicted of a felony, the First Runner-Up will assume her duties." Of course, since all of us were in our sixties, married, and living a sheltered life, we all felt pretty good about fulfilling our duties should we be elected queen.

All the speeches were immaterial, as we all unanimously elected and proudly crowned Sandra our prom queen. During the night, we danced to old tunes, revisited our many memories, and even cried a little. But to me, the highlight of the evening was when Sandra, after tugging at her dress all night, exclaimed, "I can't wait to get out of this thing!"

We had forgotten how uncomfortable formal attire could be.

Thanks for the memory, Sandra.

Postscript: It's funny how some things stick in our minds. During the limousine ride to pick up Sandra, somehow the conversation turned to gospel music, prompting Kay to spontaneously lead us in "Amazing Grace." There is something about gospel music that stays in our souls—even on prom night.

I was also touched by a comment made after we read the declaration explaining our mission stemming from Sandra's stigma that she'd never owned a prom dress. I overheard one of Sandra's daughters say, "Well, she sure bought us plenty." She was an amazing mother.

Pat leading a blindfolded Sandra to prom

Left to right: Pat, Phyllis, Kay, Sandra

The Never Ending

M any years ago, having reached an age where it was likely I might recognize the subject, I began reading the daily obituaries. At first, it was someone's parent, a church member, an elderly neighbor, or a stalwart in the community. As the years passed and the time gap tightened, it was terrifying to find classmates, friends, and relatives among the obits. Most jolting was the realization that we are all earthly mortals and subject to the same passing—a fact that escapes us during our youth. Death does not play favorites and is a 100 percent certainty. It is a sobering thought.

This daily ritual took on a new emphasis as I aged and began reading *all* the obituaries. Many times, I knew someone on the survivor list or perhaps found a mutual acquaintance among the noted careers and interests of the deceased. Some obits were quite short, and I wondered whether this person had few relatives or was a bad person; perhaps the living felt relief and a measure of good riddance. Later, newspapers began charging for lines over the first few free ones, which must have been a contributing factor. Regardless, I felt compelled to read each word in acknowledgment of the person's life. Surely, each person's time on earth has some value.

The young are the hardest to read. A life never fulfilled leaves much to wonder and speculation. Our hearts ache for the parents and siblings who will see the child never grow into an adult but, frozen in time, remain exactly as they were in the last photograph taken, framed, and given a place of honor on the mantel.

I read each obituary with interest, allowing my imagination to determine what might be hidden between the lines. Omitted, and rightly so, are the heartaches, pain, and suffering that fill any life. But also skipped over is the person's ability to overcome tragedies and find faith, comfort, and strength to move ahead. In most obituaries, there is a sense of peace at the end.

How sad that our accomplishments throughout our many years are ultimately summarized in a few short paragraphs. How is that even possible? Whom and where we came from, the schools we attended, our various careers, a list of titles, medals, and selected accomplishments, and a list of those left to cherish the memories—it's all compressed into a few short paragraphs. For many, it is the first and only time their name will appear in the newspaper.

Yet there is a great deal of sadness even when the deceased is a stranger. As we go through life's seasons, changing to fit new situations, growing, and maturing, why does it have to be over? If we could stall our life at a certain point and enjoy the present time forever, would we take that option?

So I ask, if you could go back to any time in your life and stop the clock, what time would that be? When you were a teenager wondering if someone would ask you to the prom, struggling with peer pressure, or dealing with bullies? When your children were young, night feedings, endless diaper changes, and suffering through ear infections? When your children were teenagers missing curfews and dealing with the many obstacles they face? Shuffling careers? The death of parents and loved ones? When is the perfect time to stop moving forward?

Confronted with this question, most people choose *now*, for standing still is never the answer. Unconsciously, we look forward to progressing to the next season, expecting a brighter future. Finally, we are forced to face the last and final season. This is how we are measured. This will determine the length of our obituary and how it will read. Fortunately, life's missteps are not welcome in our final reading—only the things that ultimately matter most and bring value to our lives.

An obituary is not a complete biography but a short scenario of who the person was, how they lived their life, and who is left behind to enjoy the memories. It is a time when only our goodness is acknowledged and our shortcomings are forgiven. Once we achieve death, we become perfect to those reading our obituary.

For my friend Sandra, the obituary was glowing and rightly so. She was magnanimous in spirit, true to her faith, and honest in her intentions. Daily she strived to be worthy in her own way—helpful to the less fortunate and kind to all she encountered. Once retired, she committed her time to various charities, determined to make a difference in other people's lives. "I just want to be worthy," she said to me many times.

One of the last gifts she gave me was a faceless figure by Willow Tree, hand carved by Susan Lordi. Each Willow Tree figure is representative of a feeling or one of life's events. My figure represents Happiness and is given for friendship. She resides permanently in the window above my sink with her arms spread wide. She greets me each morning with open arms and a gentle reminder that Sandra is always with me.

There are a multitude of books and psychological materials dealing with grief after the passing of a loved one. I am sure many are helpful and have brought comfort to the bereaved. I have no magic quotation or book to recommend. I can only tell you I have found that emotions are natural and should not be ignored. So if you want to cry, go ahead and cry, no matter where you are. If you suddenly think of a funny memory, go ahead and laugh, right there in the grocery store! You may find people will cry and laugh with you.

Forever be grateful this person once filled your life with joy, participated in your struggles, loved you at your worst, and as a friend was a solid influence and not just a spectator.

And most of all – keep the memories alive!

Don't walk behind me; I may not lead.
Don't walk in front of me; I may not follow.
Just walk beside me and be my friend.

—Albert Camus

THE END

Epilogue

Weeks had passed since the book had been handed over to the publisher when I discovered a touching letter I had unexpectedly received from Sandra in 2007. Going through a treasure box I keep for special cards, notes and mementos, was a tri-folded letter written on notebook paper resting in the midst of the many birthday and Mother's Day cards.

I remember being pleasantly bewildered when the letter arrived. There were no future or past occasions that would warrant personal correspondence but Sandra later explained that one particular day she felt an urge to write about our special friendship. Using the only material available at the time, her grandchildren's notebook paper, she penned the letter. It is a treasure.

Fortunately, we are able to include an exact reproduction in Sandra's beautiful handwriting which totally destroys the myth that all left-handers have poor handwriting skills. It is a lovely way to conclude the book.

My Best Friend   10/21/2007

My very first childhood friendship
began in the Summer of 1947. I
was 5 years old. The new neighbors
were moving in next door! As
I stared out the window I spotted
a little girl about my age,
skinny, not much very blonde
hair, wearing shorts and no
shirt, and sitting in the dirt
in front of the house next door.
I was so excited because now
I would have a girl to play
with!! It didn't take long —
maybe a few days or maybe
just a few hours — for me to
work my way across the "garden
yard" inch by inch. Then
we finally came face to face.
I instantly knew that this
girl would be my friend. We
were too young to realize that
this friendship would never
die — a friendship that would
last as long as we live. Her
name was Phyllis Ann Hill.
We played, we laughed, we cried,
one day at a time, never worrying
about tomorrow. We have grown
older together, knowing always that
we are just a phone call away. The
"garden yard" between us stretches

45 miles now, but we can still meet "face to face" in our thoughts and in our hearts, providing unconditional love for each other.

Sandra Lee Hass (Miller)

10/21/2007

Printed in the United States
By Bookmasters